PRACTICAL

PRINCIPLES

FOR STUDYING

THE BIBLE

Johnny A Palmer Jr.

Strength for the Study

Strength through *Power*

Strength through *Prayer*

Strength through *Presence*

Strength through battling *Prince* of darkness

Studying for the Study

Sampling from a Study

Staying with Studying

FORWARD

The Lord has allowed me to write many books but there are two, which are extremely important. One, this book, related to, How to Study the Bible and the other, called Fuel, on how to pray. If one will learn to Study God's Word and Pray, they will have their spiritual life strengthened. It is just that simple.

Chapter One

STRENGTH FOR THE STUDY

STRENGTH THROUGH *POWER*

David Huxley owns a world record pulling airplanes! On October 15, 1997, he strapped around his body a harness that was attached to a steel cable that was attached to a 747 jetliner, which weighed 187 tons. He pulled the 747 100 yards in 1 minute and 21 seconds. Often we preachers resemble that man – relying upon human resources and strength. What good is pulling a 747 a few 100 yards, when you could allow its powerful engines to fly thousands of miles into the air? And what good is preaching in our strength moving people about, when we could be empowered by the Holy Spirit to cause them to soar in the heavenlies?

[1] When I first came to you, dear brothers and sisters, I didn't use lofty words and impressive wisdom to tell you God's secret plan. [2] For I decided that while I was with you I would forget everything except Jesus Christ,

the one who was crucified. ³ I came to you in weakness—timid and trembling. ⁴ And my message and my preaching were very plain. Rather than using clever and persuasive speeches, I relied only on the power of the Holy Spirit. ⁵ I did this so you would trust not in human wisdom but in the power of God. 1 Corinthians 2:1-5

By *Renouncing Dependency* upon our *Natural* Strength. 2:1

We must not depend upon human Words.

And I, brethren, when I came to you, came not with excellency of speech – the word *excellencies* is made up of *echo* "to have" and *huper* meaning "above," it speaks of one who rises above the ordinary.

Paul's speech was not one of eloquence or superiority to the average person, or with lofty words.

¹⁰ For some say, "Paul's letters are demanding and forceful, but in person he is weak, and his speeches are worthless!" 2 Corinthians 10:10

Moses recognized the inadequacy of mere human words.

¹⁰ But Moses pleaded with the LORD, "O Lord, I'm not very good with words. I never have been, and I'm not now, even though you have spoken to me. I get tongue-tied, and my words get tangled." ¹¹ Then the LORD asked Moses, "Who makes a person's mouth? Who decides whether people speak or do not speak, hear or do not hear, see or do not see? Is it not I, the LORD? ¹² Now go! I will be with you as you speak, and I will instruct you in what to say." Exodus 4:10-12

All Christians understand this truth.

²⁶ Remember, dear brothers and sisters, that few of you were wise in the world's eyes or powerful or wealthy when God called you. ²⁷ Instead, God chose things the world considers foolish in order to shame those who think they are wise. And he chose things that are powerless to shame those who are powerful. ²⁸ God chose things despised by the world, things counted as nothing at all, and used

them to bring to nothing what the world considers important. [29] As a result, no one can ever boast in the presence of God. [30] God has united you with Christ Jesus. For our benefit God made him to be wisdom itself. Christ made us right with God; he made us pure and holy, and he freed us from sin. [31] Therefore, as the Scriptures say, "If you want to boast, boast only about the LORD."
1 Corinthians 1:26-31

D. L. Moody was greatly used by God. One news reporter went to hear him to try and find out why people were responding. The reporter wrote this in the newspaper the next day:

"Mr. Moody butchers the king's English, he has a nasal tone, an unpleasant, high-pitched voice, he is overweight and generally rough in appearance. I see nothing in Mr. Moody that would account for his success." When Moody read that, he commented, "That's the secret – there is nothing in me to account for my success."

We must not depend upon human Wisdom.

or of wisdom – this is a wisdom that is not from God.

¹⁷ For Christ didn't send me to baptize, but to preach the Good News—and not with clever speech, for fear that the cross of Christ would lose its power.
1 Corinthians 1:17

¹⁸ Stop deceiving yourselves. If you think you are wise by this world's standards, you need to become a fool to be truly wise. ¹⁹ For the wisdom of this world is foolishness to God. As the Scriptures say, "He traps the wise in the snare of their own cleverness."
1 Corinthians 3:18-19

This wisdom descends not from above, but *is* earthly, sensual, devilish. James 3:15

The word is *Sophia*; it is seen in our English word *Philosophy*. Corinth was the philosophical center of the world at that time, but Paul did not seek to convince them by way of deep philosophical speeches. It had the idea of being clever, to use great rhetorical skills. This is where one tries to give polished philosophical words to impress the listeners. Brilliant intellectual speeches with fancy words simply will not do. It's not our words or how we say them that really matters at all!

John Stott many years ago was in Sydney, Australia. The day before the final meeting, Stott received word that his father had passed away. In addition to his grief, he began losing his voice. A few hours before his time to preach he asked a few students to read 2 Cor. 12:8-9, "My grace is sufficient for you, for my strength is made perfect in weakness," and requested prayer.

He said, "I preached on the broad and narrow ways, and I had to get within half an inch of the microphone, and I croaked the gospel like a raven. I couldn't exert my personality. I couldn't move. I couldn't use any inflections in my voice. I croaked the gospel in monotone. Then when the time came to give the invitation, there was an immediate response, larger than any other meeting during the mission, as students came flocking forward."

He went on to say, "I've been back to Australia about ten times since 1958, and on every occasion somebody has come up to me and said, "Do you remember that final meeting in the university in the great hall?" "I jolly well do," I reply. "Well," they say, "I was converted that night." The Holy Spirit takes our human words, spoken in great weakness and frailty, and he carries them home with power to the mind, the heart, the conscience, and the will of the hearers in such a way that they see and believe."

We only draw upon human wisdom when we fail to draw upon God's Spirit. Why use our words and wisdom when we have His? We have the Bible, that is God's Word, and the Spirit who illuminating that Word to us!

[12] And we have received God's Spirit (not the world's spirit), so we can know the wonderful things God has

freely given us. ¹³ When we tell you these things, we do not use words that come from human wisdom. Instead, we speak words given to us by the Spirit, using the Spirit's words to explain spiritual truths.
1 Corinthians 2:12-13

By *Resolving* to *Depict* Christ as our Strength.

His *Declaration*

...declaring unto you the testimony of God – he did not bring his own message! We are living in days where personal opinion reigns as king, but the truth is nobody cares about our personal opinions, beginning with God! It is not our opinion that really matters, but what God has said in His infallible Word.

Preach the word; be instant in season, out of season; reprove, rebuke, exhort with all longsuffering and doctrine.
2 Timothy 4:2

And beginning at Moses and all the prophets, he expounded unto them in all the scriptures the things concerning Himself. Luke 24:27

Where is wisdom found? Jesus!

[1] I want you to know how much I have agonized for you and for the church at Laodicea, and for many other believers who have never met me personally. [2] I want them to be encouraged and knit together by strong ties of love. I want them to have complete confidence that they understand God's mysterious plan, which is Christ himself. [3] In him lie hidden all the treasures of wisdom and knowledge. Colossians 2:1-3

Albert Einstein was invited to speak at a banquet held in his honor at Swarthmore College. Hundreds of people from all over the country crowded an auditorium to hear what he had to say.

When it came time for him to speak, the great physicist walked to the lectern, solemnly looked around, and said, "Ladies and gentlemen, I am very sorry, but I have nothing to say." Then he sat down. The audience was in shock. A few seconds later, Einstein got up, walked back to the podium, and spoke again. "In case I have something to say, I will come back and say it." Six months later he wired the president of the college with the message: "Now I have something to say." Another dinner was held, and Einstein made his speech.

Unless we declare to people the testimony of God as found in God's Word and revealed by God's Spirit, which points people to Jesus, we really don't have anything to say either!

His *Determination*

For I determined not to know anything among you save Jesus Christ and Him crucified – everything is about Jesus!

Looking unto Jesus the author and finisher of *our* faith; who for the joy that was set before him endured the cross, despising the shame, and is set down at the right hand of the throne of God. Hebrews 12:2

[19] For the Son of God, Jesus Christ, who was preached among you by us,

even by me and Silvanus and Timotheus, was not yea and nay, but in him was yea. ²⁰ For all the promises of God in him *are* yea, and in him Amen, unto the glory of God by us.
2 Corinthians 1:19-20

⁵ For we preach not ourselves, but Christ Jesus the Lord; and ourselves your servants for Jesus' sake.
2 Corinthians 4:5

Jesus Christ is everything! We must stay focused on His Person and Work. If the church in America spent half as much time proclaiming Christ crucified as we do on the subject of politics we might see God do something!

⁴ Therefore they that were scattered abroad went every where preaching the word. ⁵ Then Philip went down to the city of Samaria, and preached Christ unto them. Acts 8:4-5

³⁵ Then Philip opened his mouth, and began at the same scripture, and preached unto him Jesus. Acts 8:35

After Paul was saved, it says "And straightway he preached Christ in the synagogues, that he is the Son of God (Acts 9:20). We must determine to focus on Jesus Christ not a denomination; not some celebrity or preacher! I'm told that one man went to one church after another listening to the great preachers of his day. He left one church after another saying, "What a preacher! What a preacher! Then he heard Charles Spurgeon and said, "Oh my, what a Savior!"

Tozer, "The Christian's interests have shifted from self to Christ. What he is, or is not, no longer concerns him…Christ is now where the man's ego was formerly. The man is now Christ-centered instead of self-centered, and he forgets himself in his delighted preoccupation with Christ."

Lloyd-Jones, "Pride is ever the cause of trouble, and there is nothing that so hurts the natural man's pride as the cross of Christ. How does the cross do that? What happened that there should ever have been a cross? It is because we are failures, because we are sinners, because we are lost. The Christian is not a good man. He is a vile wretch who has been saved by the grace of God."

We must focus on what's really important! It reminds me of a prosperous Bank *owner* who just purchased a brand new Rolls-Royce. He went around a corner too fast and was thrown out of the car. His car smashed into a tree and burst into flames. The man was alive but his arm had been ripped off. A truck driver stopped to help the man. The rich man cried out, "Oh, my brand new Rolls-Royce! The Truck driver said, "Sir you have a bigger problem than that – your arm is gone!" The rich man noticing his arm was missing cried out, "Oh, my new Rolex!" Many times we are like that Banker we don't understand what's really important! It is not the offering; or the size of the church; or the eloquence of the pastor – it is Jesus Christ that's important!

By *Realizing* the *Deficiency* of our Strength.

He was *Sick*. [Tired, in Distress]

I was with you in weakness – this word can be translated sickness. Paul did not enjoy good health!

13 Surely you remember that I was sick when I first brought you the Good News. 14 But even though my condition tempted you to reject me, you did not despise me or turn me away. No, you took me in and cared for me as though I were an angel from God or even Christ Jesus himself. Galatians 4:13-14

7 even though I have received such wonderful revelations from God. So to keep me from becoming proud, I was given a thorn in my flesh, a messenger from Satan to torment me and keep me from becoming proud. 8 Three different times I begged the Lord to take it away. 9 Each time he said, "My grace is all you need. My power works best in weakness." So now I am glad to boast about my weaknesses, so that the power of Christ can work through me. 10 That's why I take pleasure in my weaknesses, and in the insults, hardships, persecutions, and troubles that I suffer for Christ. For when I am

weak, then I am strong.
2 Corinthians 12:7-10

American Christianity is obsessed with physical health these days – everything is about exercising; eating right; and taking vitamins; and watching one's cholesterol level. We have forgotten, "But we have this treasure in earthen vessels, that the excellency of the power may be of God, and not of us." 2 Corinthians 4:7

Suffering sickness is designed to drive us to God's strength! One puritan prayed, "Lord, you show your power by my frailty, so that the more feeble I am, the more fit to be used, for You pitch a tent of grace in my weakness. Help me to rejoice in my infirmities and give You praise, to acknowledge my deficiencies before others and not be discouraged by them, that they may see Your glory more clearly."

And I can tell you from personal experience, the older you get the more sickness you will experience!

[1] Don't let the excitement of youth cause you to forget your Creator.

Honor him in your youth before you grow old and say, "Life is not pleasant anymore." ² Remember him before the light of the sun, moon, and stars is dim to your old eyes, and rain clouds continually darken your sky. ³ Remember him before your legs—the guards of your house—start to tremble; and before your shoulders—the strong men—stoop. Remember him before your teeth—your few remaining servants—stop grinding; and before your eyes—the women looking through the windows—see dimly. ⁴ Remember him before the door to life's opportunities is closed and the sound of work fades. Now you rise at the first chirping of the birds, but then all their sounds will grow faint. ⁵ Remember him before you become fearful of falling and worry about danger in the streets; before your hair turns white like an almond tree in bloom, and you drag along without energy like a dying grasshopper, and the caperberry no longer inspires sexual desire. Remember him before you near the grave, your everlasting home, when the mourners will weep at your funeral. Ecclesiastes 12:1-5

For which cause we faint not; but though our outward man perish, yet the inward *man* is renewed day by day. 2 Corinthians 4:16

James H. Brookes said, "Sickness is a rough but thorough teacher of experimental theology, and it almost compels the soul of the believer to stay itself upon God."

There is the Edinburgh Castle in Scotland. That beautiful castle was protected on every side except one. On one side is a great cliff that goes up, and they knew that no enemy could take it there. But, history declares that on that impregnable rock side is where the castle was taken. Not at its place of weakness, but at its place of strength. Do you know what the trouble is with many of us – our supposed places of strength! And that's why God often allows sickness because it causes us to distrust our human strength.

He was *Scared.* [Timid, in Dread]

and in fear – faith doesn't eliminate fear, it simply refuses to be stopped by it!

5 For, when we were come into Macedonia, our flesh had no rest, but we were troubled on every side; without *were* fightings, within *were* fears. 2 Corinthians 7:5

Brian Harbour, *Rising Above the Crowd,* writes:

"Fear can at times be a positive motivator. Fear is behind every notable achievement of mankind. Fear of ignorance led to the public school system; Fear of disease led to medical research; Fear of darkness led to the development of the electric light; Fear of exposure led to the construction of houses; Fear is at times an instructor. Fear at its best summons forth new energies, produces life's most valuable achievements, and protects from life's severest hazards."

Fear that drives us to brokenness and dependency upon God is a good thing. Too often we're like the preacher who had a great sermon, he knew he was going to impress them and ascended into the pulpit with great confidence. But his mind went blank! After a few minutes of stammering around he sat down. He asked a fellow preacher what happened. And he was told, "If you would have ascended into the pulpit, like you descended from it, you would have been a blessing to them.

He was a bit *Shaky*. [Trembling, in Doubt]

and in much trembling- there is nothing wrong with trembling if it drives us to depend upon God's power!

Wherefore, my beloved, as ye have always obeyed, not as in my presence only, but now much more in my absence, work out your own salvation with fear and trembling. Philippians 2:12

Charles Spurgeon wrote, "Under a sense of the presence of God, we tremble lest we should sin, we tremble lest that presence should remove, lest we should grieve the Spirit and vex the holy One of Israel...It is no child's play, but an awful weighty business. I pray

God we may know more of holy trembling, that the awful majesty of divine love may be so revealed to us that we may lie prostrate beneath its force..."

Being entrusted to preach the Word of God is not child's play, may we have a godly dread of not glorifying God as we should...Do we realize our inability to preach?

5 "Yes, I am the vine; you are the branches. Those who remain in me, and I in them, will produce much fruit. For apart from me you can do nothing. John 15:5

By *Relying* upon *Divine Supernatural* Strength

A Denunciation

And my speech and my preaching was not with enticing words of man's wisdom – again we must denounce dependency upon our human resources.

5 It is not that we think we are qualified to do anything on our own. Our qualification comes from God. 6

He has enabled us to be ministers of his new covenant. This is a covenant not of written laws, but of the Spirit. The old written covenant ends in death; but under the new covenant, the Spirit gives life. 2 Corinthians 3:5-6

Many have swallowed Satan's lie that feeling inadequate keeps us from being used by God – it is actually the basis of being used.

Mephibosheth called himself a "dead dog" and yet had a place at the kings table (2 Sam. 9:6-13);

Gideon had to confess that he was "least in my father's house." (Jud. 6:15);

The turning point came in *Job's life* when he "abhorred himself." (Job. 42:6);

Moses had it right when he said, "Who am I that I should go to Pharoah?" (Ex. 3:11);

Paul confessed he "was nothing" (2 Cor. 12:11), and "the least of all the saints" (Eph. 3:8), and the "chief of sinners" (1 Tim. 1:15).

Donald Barnhouse, "If you exalt man in any way, God is thereby debased. But if you exalt God as He should be exalted, man thereby takes his true position of utter nothingness, and only then can he find his real exaltation, for it will come to him through the grace of God in Christ."

As long as our Inadequacy draws us to His Sufficiency everything is as it should be. Reminds me of a Lady in a yarn factory, it was her first day on the job. Her supervisor told her, "If, the yarn starts to get tangled, do not try to untangle it, just come and get me. Well it was not long before it began to be tangled, and so she tried to untangle it by herself. Before long there was a huge ball of tangled yarn going everywhere. The supervisor came by and saw it, and said, "My, what a mess!" She cried out, "I did the best I could." He said, "No, if you would have done the best you could, you would have come to me." We do our best only when we draw upon the Lord's sufficiency.

A *Demonstration*

but in demonstration of the Spirit and of power- Paul's source of power was God's Spirit!

[18] Yet I dare not boast about anything except what Christ has done through me, bringing the Gentiles to God by my message and by the way I worked among them. [19] They were convinced by the power of miraculous signs and wonders and by the power of God's Spirit. In this way, I have fully presented the Good News of Christ from Jerusalem all the way to Illyricum. Romans 15:18-19

[5] For when we brought you the Good News, it was not only with words but also with power, for the Holy Spirit gave you full assurance that what we said was true. And you know of our concern for you from the way we lived when we were with you.
1 Thessalonians 1:5

There was a preacher in Kentucky who used to keep on his desk an old tattered leather glove; and each Sunday, before he'd go out to preach, he took that old glove off of the desk, and he would slip his hand into the glove and flex it several times. Then he would take the glove off, put it on his desk, and go preach. Someone said, "Why do you do that?" He said, "To remind myself of this vital lesson that that glove is absolutely impotent and powerless until my hand is slipped into it, and then I say, 'O God, as my hand has activated this glove, I want you, Lord Jesus, to activate my life, and I want you, Lord, to enter into me and inhabit my humanity and live Your life through me.'"

A *Design*

that your faith should not stand in the wisdom of men but in the power of God – it is God not us, who is the object of our faith.

Charles Swindoll, "Why didn't Paul take speech lessons from the expert communicators of his day? Why didn't he try to throw in some clever lines, entertaining jokes, or spellbinding arguments to wow his audience? Because he wanted God's power, not human wisdom, to convince the Corinthians to accept the truth."

Showing forth the Spirit's Strength in our Study. That means no gimmicks, no lofty words, just a plain and simple dependency upon Almighty God! I am not a big man, but I can lift a 1,000 lbs! You say that's impossible. It is if I limited myself to this realm – you're right. But if I get on a *Space Shuttle* and travel to another realm, into outer space I can easily lift a 1,000 lbs. If we limit ourselves to the physical realm there is not a person in this room who can rightly give a sermon that will have an eternal impact; but if we draw upon the spiritual realm, we can do all things through Christ who strengthens us.

Chapter Two

STRENGTH THROUGH *PRAYER*

Robert McCheyne was offered many influential and prestigious positions but he always turned them down. His reasoning was, "No church can offer me more time for prayer." One of the great advantages about pastoring a small church is that it affords the pastor more time for prayer, and thus a more powerful pulpit ministry.

I want us to turn our attention to two passages of Scriptures:

16 Confess your sins to each other and pray for each other so that you may be healed. The earnest prayer of a righteous person has great power and produces wonderful results. 17 Elijah was as human as we are, and yet when he prayed earnestly that no rain would fall, none fell for three and a half years! 18 Then, when he prayed again, the sky sent down rain and the earth began to yield its crops. 19 My dear brothers and sisters, if someone among you wanders away from the truth and is brought back, 20 you can be sure that whoever brings the sinner back will save that person from death

and bring about the forgiveness of many sins. James 5:16-20

⁴¹ Then Elijah said to Ahab, "Go get something to eat and drink, for I hear a mighty rainstorm coming!" ⁴² So Ahab went to eat and drink. But Elijah climbed to the top of Mount Carmel and bowed low to the ground and prayed with his face between his knees. ⁴³ Then he said to his servant, "Go and look out toward the sea." The servant went and looked, then returned to Elijah and said, "I didn't see anything." Seven times Elijah told him to go and look. ⁴⁴ Finally the seventh time, his servant told him, "I saw a little cloud about the size of a man's hand rising from the sea." Then Elijah shouted, "Hurry to Ahab and tell him, 'Climb into your chariot and go back home. If you don't hurry, the rain will stop you!'" ⁴⁵ And soon the sky was black with clouds. A heavy wind brought a terrific rainstorm, and Ahab left quickly for Jezreel. ⁴⁶ Then the LORD gave special strength to Elijah. He tucked his cloak into his belt and ran ahead of Ahab's chariot all the way

to the entrance of Jezreel. 1 Kings 18:41-46

The prayer *Request*

The effectual fervent prayer - it all begins with prayer. We are not talking about talking about prayer or reading books about prayer, but actually praying.

"...yet you have not, because you ask not." James 4:2

Gilbert Jesse Brown, a former nose tackle who played for the Green Bay Packers, was a highly sought after free agent after the 1996 season; In spite of a pay cut he decided to stay with the Packers. Jacksonville offered him an extra million dollars to put his 325 pound body into their uniform, but Brown decided to stay in Green Bay. Why would he turn down a million dollars? It is because a tearful little girl during an autograph signing asked him to stay. Many times God doesn't answer our prayers because we simply haven't prayed!

The prayer *Requirement*

of a righteous man - our foundation is the imputed righteousness of Christ, without that, God would not answer anyone's prayers (Jn. 14:6). As that great hymn goes, "My hope is built on nothing less than Jesus' blood and righteousness; I dare not trust the sweetest frame but wholly lean on Jesus' name." But we are also to build upon that imputed righteousness with imparted righteousness – this happens as we say *no* to self and *yes* to God's Spirit. We cannot hold onto sin and have an effective prayer life!

Ye ask, and receive not, because ye ask amiss, that ye may consume *it* upon your lusts. James 4:3

Sin is like spiritual kryptonite!

Remember Superman? He had all of those wonderful powers, but he was weak as a kitten in the presence of kryptonite. God has wonderful power to be released to and through us, but sin blocks God's power and weakens us.

The *Results* of Prayer

God is *Working* - Things Happen!

The effective, fervent - this is viewed by many as a passive voice, meaning it is God doing the working not us. We get our word *energy* from this word. The result of prayer is that it releases the energy of God Himself! He works, accomplishes things, and brings results, when we pray for that *lost person* God begins to work. We lift up that *wayward child* God begins to work. And the lists goes on and on, but understand God always works in His way, according to His timetable, and in a way that will be eternally profitable even if it doesn't look like it in time.

The bottom line is that when we pray God makes things happen! We often have to accept this by faith not by sight (2 Cor. 5:7).

The murder rate in New York City dropped significantly in the last ten years, and a primary reason is prayer. A New York City policeman recently told a group of British Christians that since the introduction of a 24-hour prayer clock a decade ago the annual murder caseload has fallen from 2,600 to 600. Detective Donald Sanchez said, "Some of the credit could go to former Mayor Giuliani's tough stand on crime, but God is sovereign. He places people in office and government."

God gives *Winning* - it brings Tremendous Help!

availeth much - the word means "to prevail, to overcome." Prayer releases God's power to overcome much opposition. It is through prayer that self and Satan are resisted! The nuclear submarine *Thresher* had heavy steel armor, so it could dive deep and withstand the pressure of the ocean. Unfortunately, on a test run in 1963, the *Thresher's* nuclear engine quit, and it could not get back to the surface. It sank deeper and deeper into the ocean. The pressure became immense. The heavy steel bulkheads buckled; the *Thresher* was crushed with 129 people inside. The Navy searched for the *Thresher* with a research craft that was much stronger than submarines. It was shaped like a steel ball and was lowered into the ocean on a cable. They finally located the *Thresher* at a depth of 8,400 feet: one and a half miles down. It was crushed like an egg shell. What was surprising to the searchers was that they saw fish at that great depth. And these fish did not have inches of steel to protect them. They appeared to have normal skin, a fraction of an inch thick. How can these fish survive under all that pressure? They have a secret. Their secret is that they have the same pressure inside themselves as they have on the outside. Survival under pressure! Sounds like a good title for a movie or book or something. Prayer enables us to prevail over great satanic pressure because "Greater is He who is in us, then he that is in the world!"

Prayer *Reflection*

17 Elias was a man subject to like passions as we are, and he prayed earnestly that it might not rain: and it rained not on the earth by the space of three years and six months. 18 And he prayed again, and the heaven gave rain, and the earth brought forth her

fruit. ¹⁹ Brethren, if any of you do err from the truth, and one convert him; James 5:17-19

The *Prayer*

He was Just like us! He was subject to like passions as we are, here is one of the most powerful men in the O.T., yet he was just a human being! He had a sin nature just like we do. If God can work mightily in and through Elijah, then He can work mightily in and through us.

He Just prayed! We find no secret formula; no magic potion. He simply prayed.

The *Power*

It did not rain for three years and six months! Now let's turn to 1 Kings 18:41-46, and take a closer look.

Prayer can be offered by one *solitary person.*

"And Elijah said unto Ahab, Get up, eat and drink; for there is a sound of abundance of rain. God is going to answer prayer through one man -

Elijah. Ahab can go eat and drink or whatever, he has no heart for God. Notice God does not need a committee or even a group of believers serious about God to get things going - He needs just one person! One with God is a majority!

"...The effective, fervent prayer of a righteous man [singular] can accomplish much. James 5:16

30 And I sought for a man among them, that should make up the hedge, and stand in the gap before me for the land, that I should not destroy it: but I found none. 31 Therefore have I poured out mine indignation upon them; I have consumed them with the fire of my wrath: their own way have I recompensed upon their heads, says the Lord GOD. Ezekiel 22:30-31

"Give me a man of God – one man,

One mighty prophet of the Lord,

And I will give you peace on earth,

Bought with a prayer and not a sword." [Gordon Liddell]

Henry Varley once said to D. L. Moody, "The world has yet to see what God can do with and for and through and in a man who is fully and wholly consecrated to Him." Moody prayed, "O Lord, let me be that man!" History has proven this to be true. Time after time God raised up just one man to bring forth revival - George Whitefield; Charles Spurgeon; D. L. Moody; John Wesley; Martin Luther; Billy Graham....

Lloyd-Jones, "Let us get out of this deplorable modern habit which makes the ordinary church member think that he or she can do nothing...No, the teaching of the Bible is the exact opposite; it may be *you* that God is going to use. Therefore, I am entitled to ask - have you got a zeal for the glory of God? If this is a burden that can come to anybody, why has it not come to you?"

Prayer requires *spiritual perception*

"for there is a sound of abundance of rain." There is no indication that he heard a physical sound. That came

later. Faith is evidence of things not seen! (Heb. 11:1, 6)

It is vital to realize that faith begins with a word from God.

So then faith *comes* by hearing, and hearing by the word of God. Romans 10:17

13 For this cause also thank we God without ceasing, because, when you received the word of God which you heard of us, you received *it* not *as* the word of men, but as it is in truth, the word of God, which effectually worked also in you that believe.
1 Thessalonians 2:13

Elijah clearly had such a word, "1 And it came to pass *after* many days, that the word of the LORD came to Elijah in the third year, saying, Go, show yourself unto Ahab; and I will send rain upon the earth. 1 Kings 18:1

What word do we have? Jam. 5:16-17! Do we really believe that promise? Driving southbound on Interstate 5 in Valencia, CA, the home of Six Flags Magic Mountain, is a large Disneyland billboard with a single word dominating 75% of the space. The word? Believe! Disney is asking the public to suspend their disbelief for a time and enter into their enchanted Kingdom for a day of recreation. They want us to pretend, for a time that "make believe" is worth believing in. God's kingdom is *not* make believe, it is really real! And God is asking only one thing from us - Believe!

Tozer, "[Our basic problem] is our chronic unbelief. Faith enables our spiritual sense to function. Where faith is defective the result will be inward insensibility and numbness toward spiritual things. This is the condition of vast numbers of Christians today. A spiritual kingdom lies all about us, enclosing us, embracing us, altogether within reach of our inner selves, waiting for us to recognize it. God Himself is here waiting our response to His presence. The eternal world will come alive to us the moment we begin to reckon upon its reality."

Prayer requires *spiritual passion*

"So Ahab went up to eat and to drink. And Elijah went up to the top of Carmel; and he cast himself down upon the earth, and put his face between his knees." If you get down on your knees to pray and put your face between your knees you have effectively blocked out everything but God! We cannot watch TV, read secular books, listen to music that feeds the flesh and do business with God!

24 "No one can serve two masters. For you will hate one and love the other; you will be devoted to one and despise the other. You cannot serve both God and money. Matthew 6:24

6 But let him ask in faith, nothing wavering. For he that wavers is like a wave of the sea driven with the wind and tossed. 7 For let not that man think that he shall receive any thing of the Lord. 8 A double minded man *is* unstable in all his ways. James 1:6-8

No double-minded man will ever experience revival! We are to seek God with all our heart...it demands our full attention. The people of Elijah's day were distracted with Baal worship.

And Elijah came unto all the people, and said, How long halt ye between two opinions? if the LORD *be* God, follow him: but if Baal, *then* follow him. And the people answered him not a word. 1 Kings 18:21

Someone said, "Let water spread over the real estate, and you have a stagnant swamp. Channel it, and you can have a power dam. Diffuse light and it spreads over this auditorium. Concentrate it—it becomes a laser that can burn through steel. Concentration —everything else has to become subservient to your master goal."

Paul said, "[13] Brethren, I count not myself to have apprehended: but *this* one thing *I do*, forgetting those things which are behind, and reaching forth unto those things which are before, [14] I press toward the mark for the prize of the high calling of God in Christ Jesus." Philippians 3:13-14

Ernest Hemingway's life went in many directions. He won a Pulitzer Prize. He won a Nobel Prize. He was a news reporter—when World War I began; He was a big game hunter; He was a bullfighter; He was a fisherman; When World War II came, he took his fishing boat and rigged it with two 50-caliber machine guns, bazookas, hand grenades, and would cruise off the coast of Cuba, hoping that a German U-boat would surface; He was in an airplane accident; He was hit by a taxi; He was wounded in war. He lived in France; Italy; Cuba; in Key West; and in Idaho. He was a man that did just about everything, even authored, you name it.

But, he was a distracted man - he lacked any meaningful purpose; he lacked being focused on one thing. As a result, he was enslaved to, and abused alcohol; He went through four marriages. He said, finally, at the end of all of this, thinking of his life, "It seems that we are ants on the end of a burning log." One day he ended it all by putting a shotgun to his head! A meaningful life excludes a thousand distractions and focuses its attention on God!

Prayer is made by those who are *spiritually positive*

"And said to his servant, Go up now, look toward the sea." Why? He is looking for his prayers to be answered! He is expecting something to happen. Do we?

7 Ask, and it shall be given you; seek, and you shall find; knock, and it shall be opened unto you: 8 For every one that asks receives; and he that seeks finds; and to him that knocks it shall be opened. Matthew 7:7-8

24 You haven't done this before. Ask, using my name, and you will receive, and you will have abundant joy. John 16:24

14 And this is the confidence that we have in him, that, if we ask any thing according to his will, he hears us: 15 And if we know that he hear us, whatsoever we ask, we know that we have the petitions that we desired of him.   1 John 5:14-15

When a mother is with child what do we say? We say "She's Expecting!"

She doesn't know exactly when, but she is expecting that baby to be born. Every believer should be "Expecting!" Expecting God to give birth to that prayer. Do we really expect someone to be saved? Any visitors? New members? Revival?

Prayer often encounters *spiritual postponements*

"And he went up and looked and said, There is nothing" - this is where most quit! We tend to say see it doesn't work! But it is normal to have the answer delayed! Daniel prayed 3 weeks before God answered his prayers…The Psalmist often wonders why God delays in answering prayer…Psa. 10:1; 13:1; 55:1-3; 69:17; 77:2-3, 7-8; 88:9, 13-14

That is why you have to walk by Fact, then Faith, then Feelings! Watchman Nee, "We *must* believe God no matter how convincing Satan's arguments appear…He resorts to lying feelings and experiences in his attempts to shake us from our faith in God's Word…So we must choose. Will we believe Satan's lie or God's truth? Are we going to be governed by appearances or by what God says?...Faith is always meeting a mountain, a mountain of evidence that seems to contradict God's Word, a mountain of apparent contradictions...either faith or the mountain has to go." God says, "The fervent effective prayer of a righteous man accomplishes much" are we going to believe that or these empty pews? Fact, faith, and experience were walking along the top of a building. Fact walked steadily onward - looking neither to the right or the left; Faith followed - keeping its eyes firmly on Fact. All went well...Until Faith was concerned about Experience - so he took his eyes off Fact and turned to see how *he* was getting on, and lost his balance and fell off the wall.

Prayer requires *spiritual perseverance*

"And he said, go again seven times" - Seven times he told his servant go back and see if anything is happening

yet. We must persist in prayer until God answers!

5 Then, teaching them more about prayer, he used this story: "Suppose you went to a friend's house at midnight, wanting to borrow three loaves of bread. You say to him, 6 'A friend of mine has just arrived for a visit, and I have nothing for him to eat.' 7 And suppose he calls out from his bedroom, 'Don't bother me. The door is locked for the night, and my family and I are all in bed. I can't help you.' 8 But I tell you this—though he won't do it for friendship's sake, if you keep knocking long enough, he will get up and give you whatever you need because of your shameless persistence. 9 "And so I tell you, keep on asking, and you will receive what you ask for. Keep on seeking, and you will find. Keep on knocking, and the door will be opened to you. 10 For everyone who asks, receives. Everyone who seeks, finds. And to everyone who knocks, the door will be opened.
Luke 11:5-10

¹ One day Jesus told his disciples a story to show that they should always pray and never give up. ² "There was a judge in a certain city," he said, "who neither feared God nor cared about people. ³ A widow of that city came to him repeatedly, saying, 'Give me justice in this dispute with my enemy.' ⁴ The judge ignored her for a while, but finally he said to himself, 'I don't fear God or care about people, ⁵ but this woman is driving me crazy. I'm going to see that she gets justice, because she is wearing me out with her constant requests!'" ⁶ Then the Lord said, "Learn a lesson from this unjust judge. ⁷ Even he rendered a just decision in the end. So don't you think God will surely give justice to his chosen people who cry out to him day and night? Will he keep putting them off? ⁸ I tell you, he will grant justice to them quickly! But when the Son of Man returns, how many will he find on the earth who have faith?" Luke 18:1-8

When Jacob wrestled with the Angel of the Lord, they wrestled all night and finally the Angel of the Lord said, "I'm leaving!" And Jacob held on and said, "I'm not letting go until you bless me!" For sixty years the members of Oak Grove Baptist Church in Mount Carmel, TN prayed for Joe Arnott to come to Christ. Even though he wasn't a Christian, he was a religious man and attended Sunday School and Church for all those years, but never accepted Christ as his Savior and Lord. Several church members witnessed to him, but his answer was always the same, "I'm not ready yet." No one gave up, they kept praying for him. March 5, 2000 their prayers were answered. Arnott made a public profession of his faith. The congregation wept as they watched sixty years of prayers walk the isle to give his life to Jesus. Seeing what was happening, the men in his Sunday School class followed Arnott down the aisle and stood with him as he made his decision. His pastor, Benny Keck said, "I suppose fewer words will ever sound sweeter to my ears than hearing Joe say, 'I believe that Jesus is the Christ, the Son of the Living God."

Prayer rejoices in any *spiritual progress*

"And it came to pass at the seventh time, that he said, Behold, there ariseth a little cloud out of the sea, like a man's hand" - just a small cloud! But enough to encourage Elijah!

9 "Zerubbabel is the one who laid the foundation of this Temple, and he will complete it. Then you will know that the LORD of Heaven's Armies has sent me. 10 Do not despise these small beginnings, for the LORD rejoices to see the work begin, to see the plumb line in Zerubbabel's hand." (The seven lamps represent the eyes of the LORD that search all around the world.) Zechariah 4:9-10

Charles Spurgeon preached to thousands in London each Lord's Day, yet he started his ministry by accepting invitations to preach in obscure places in the country side. He said, "I am perfectly sure, that, if I had not been willing to preach to those small gatherings of people in obscure country places, I should never have had the privilege of preaching to thousands of men and women in large buildings all over the land."

Little is much, when God is in it!

Prayer is not afraid to make a *spiritual profession*

"And he said, Go up, say unto Ahab, Prepare thy chariot, and get thee down, that the rain stop thee not. - remember they were in a three year drought! Nothing in the sky but a small cloud!

Anybody can confess God is going to do something after He has done it! But what about a preacher who gets up when there is only a handful of members and says, "I am trusting God to bring a down-pour of revival." Satan whispers in my ear, "Hey, you better shut up about this revival stuff. You have been in a drought for many years. Nothing has happened – you are beginning to look like a fool! Genuine faith will take that chance! It will put oneself in a position where if God doesn't come through, you're through! And you will look like a fool.

Moses went to the children of Israel and said that God had promised them deliverance from Egyptian bondage, and things only got worse!

[1] After this presentation to Israel's leaders, Moses and Aaron went and spoke to Pharaoh. They told him, "This is what the LORD, the God of Israel, says: Let my people go so they may hold a festival in my honor in the wilderness." [2] "Is that so?" retorted Pharaoh. "And who is the LORD? Why should I listen to him and let Israel go? I don't know the LORD, and I will not let Israel go." Exodus 5:1-2

[6] That same day Pharaoh sent this order to the Egyptian slave drivers and the Israelite foremen: [7] "Do not supply any more straw for making bricks. Make the people get it themselves! [8] But still require them to make the same number of bricks as before. Don't reduce the quota. They are lazy. That's why they are crying out, 'Let us go and offer sacrifices to our God.' Exodus 5:6-8

[19] The Israelite foremen could see that they were in serious trouble when they were told, "You must not reduce the number of bricks you make each day." [20] As they left Pharaoh's court, they confronted Moses and Aaron, who were waiting outside for them. [21] The foremen said to them, "May the LORD judge and punish you for making us stink before Pharaoh and his officials. You have put a sword into their hands, an excuse to kill us!" [22] Then Moses went back to the LORD and protested, "Why have you brought all this trouble on your own people, Lord? Why did you send me? [23] Ever since I came to Pharaoh as your spokesman, he has been even more brutal to your people. And you have done nothing to rescue them!" Exodus 5:19-23

But Moses persisted on confessing to the people and to Pharaoh what God had promised! And through 10 mighty plagues Israel was delivered from Egyptian bondage.

Answered prayer will mean *spiritual downpour, "And it came to pass in the mean while, that the heaven was black with clouds and wind, and there was a great rain. And Ahab rode, and went to Jezreel.* - it was a heavy down-pour. God always gives us more then we ask for!

Call unto me, and I will answer thee, and show you great and mighty things, which you know not. Jeremiah 33:3

[20] Now all glory to God, who is able, through his mighty power at work within us, to accomplish infinitely more than we might ask or think. [21] Glory to him in the church and in Christ Jesus through all generations forever and ever! Amen. Ephesians 3:20-21

When Jesus turned the water into wine the Bible scholars tell us it was 120 gallons! More than they could ever need.

With God the cup overflows! Psa. 23:5

When Jesus fed the 5000 with a little boy's sack lunch, there were 12 full baskets left over.

He doesn't just give peace, but peace that passes all understanding."

He doesn't just give joy, but "joy unspeakable and full of glory (1 Pet. 1:8).

When the Prodigal Son came back he said, "bring the fatted calf!...the best robe!"

He doesn't give life – He gives life more abundantly.

Prayer brings *spiritual power*

"And the hand of the LORD was on Elijah; and he girded up his loins, and ran before Ahab to the entrance of Jezreel." - God's hand was on Elijah! The powerful presence of God is the great result of answered Prayer!

6 This Ezra was a scribe who was well versed in the Law of Moses, which the LORD, the God of Israel, had given to the people of Israel. He came up to Jerusalem from Babylon, and the king gave him everything he asked for, because the gracious hand of the LORD his God was on him. 7 Some of the people of Israel, as well as some of the priests, Levites, singers, gatekeepers, and Temple servants,

traveled up to Jerusalem with him in the seventh year of King Artaxerxes' reign. ⁸ Ezra arrived in Jerusalem in August of that year. ⁹ He had arranged to leave Babylon on April 8, the first day of the new year, and he arrived at Jerusalem on August 4, for the gracious hand of his God was on him.
Ezra 7:6-9

²⁸ And praise him for demonstrating such unfailing love to me by honoring me before the king, his council, and all his mighty nobles! I felt encouraged because the gracious hand of the LORD my God was on me. And I gathered some of the leaders of Israel to return with me to Jerusalem.
Ezra 7:28

¹⁸ And by the *good hand of our God upon us* they brought us a man of understanding, of the sons of Mahli, the son of Levi, the son of Israel; and Sherebiah, with his sons and his brethren, eighteen; ²² For I was ashamed to require of the king a band of soldiers and horsemen to help us against the enemy in the way: because we had spoken unto the king, saying,

The hand of our God is upon all them for good that seek him; but his power and his wrath *is* against all them that forsake him. ³¹ Then we departed from the river of Ahava on the twelfth *day* of the first month, to go unto Jerusalem: and *the hand of our God was upon us*, and he delivered us from the hand of the enemy, and of such as lay in wait by the way. Ezra 8:18, 22, 31 See Psa. 139:5-10 and Ac. 1:8.

It is that intimacy with God's *face* that keeps His hand upon us! The flesh will whimper and Satan will fight us every step of the way. It's easy to get into God's manifested presence, its constant warfare to stay there! Imagine if you were invited to a dinner gala at Buckingham Palace with Queen Elizabeth II. You would follow protocol, bow in her presence; dress properly; follow the rules of etiquette; etc. It would be fun and exciting, but how would you like to live there! To stay dressed up all the time and to properly behave yourself 24/7. We want to put on those old torn blue jeans; wear those nasty but comfortable boots; eat our food like a hog; we don't want to live by the Queen's rules every day. To experience God's manifested presence is like that, our old sin nature will not like it! It doesn't want to bow; it doesn't like to live in a manner proper to the King; it wants to break the rules and sin; Satan hates the thought because, for the first time in your life, supernatural, unexplainable things will begin to happen that destroys his kingdom.

Tozer, "To enter that awesome presence means we have to live right. That is why the average Christian is perfectly willing to wait for heaven to have the experience of always being in the [manifested] presence of God. I think that if the average Christian would tell the truth from the depth of his heart, he would have to admit that being in the [manifested] presence of God all the time [would take more effort and discipline then he really wants to put forth]. He wants to escape to the world and the flesh, like the children of Israel he longs for the fleshpots of Egypt. It is just too much of a demand of us, that we go into the land and stay there. Yet that is what the Holy Spirit is pleading that we do." So we cop out and say, "Well, nobody's perfect! I'm not under the law, even though God says the law is written in our hearts, I'm under grace and am free to do as I please - and Satan gives us a false manifestation so as to deceive us...We want a revival that we can put on our calendar for Sunday through Thursday! That is not what I'm talking about. Although I am certainly not belittling that, many times such a meeting has been used by God to bring genuine revival.

Spiritual Strength of the Study relates to prayer. We have the Fact of Jam. 5:16, now all we have to do is apply it by Faith, and one day Experience will follow. A. C. Dickson said, "When we depend upon organization, we get what organization can do, and that's something; When we depend upon education, we get what education can do, and that is something. When we depend upon money, we get what money can do, and that is something; When we depend upon singing and preaching, we get what they can do, and that is something." But, when we depend upon prayer, we will get what God can do - [and that is Awesome!] What all the churches; and all the homes; and all the schools; and all the individuals need is what God can do; How shall we get what God can do? By prayer, out of hearts, that are right with God."

Chapter Three

STRENGTHENED THROUGH GOD'S *PRESENCE*

We talk about real revival; it is a manifestation of God's Presence, which is equivalent to God's power. The two are in reality inseparable (Ac. 1:8).

In the book Revival Fire, we find these words:

"During revival people are moved toward Christ, people who can be moved in no other way. Many prayers that have gone unanswered for years are gloriously answered. Often the very atmosphere seems awesomely filled with God's power. Christians recognize it as the holy presence of

God...There may be such a sense of God's presence and power that some people tremble. Some may be moved to weeping before God; some at times sink to the ground in physical helplessness. Others may feel almost irresistibly drawn to attend revival services or to convene at a place and time where no service has been announced...All these divine manifestations have been marked by an unusually widespread awareness of God's presence, God's mercy, and God's transforming power in the lives of people."

7 It was Moses' practice to take the Tent of Meeting and set it up some distance from the camp. Everyone who wanted to make a request of the LORD would go to the Tent of Meeting outside the camp. 8 Whenever Moses went out to the Tent of Meeting, all the people would get up and stand in the entrances of their own tents. They would all watch Moses until he disappeared inside. 9 As he went into the tent, the pillar of cloud would come down and hover at its entrance while the LORD spoke with Moses. 10 When

the people saw the cloud standing at the entrance of the tent, they would stand and bow down in front of their own tents. 11 Inside the Tent of Meeting, the LORD would speak to Moses face to face, as one speaks to a friend. Afterward Moses would return to the camp, but the young man who assisted him, Joshua son of Nun, would remain behind in the Tent of Meeting. 12 One day Moses said to the LORD, "You have been telling me, 'Take these people up to the Promised Land.' But you haven't told me whom you will send with me. You have told me, 'I know you by name, and I look favorably on you.' 13 If it is true that you look favorably on me, let me know your ways so I may understand you more fully and continue to enjoy your favor. And remember that this nation is your very own people." 14 The LORD replied, "I will personally go with you, Moses, and I will give you rest— everything will be fine for you." 15 Then Moses said, "If you don't personally go with us, don't make us leave this place. 16 How will anyone know that you look favorably on me—

on me and on your people—if you don't go with us? For your presence among us sets your people and me apart from all other people on the earth." Exodus 33:7-16

Moses' *Isolation*

His *Priority*

Moses dropped everything on his schedule and got alone with God. A man called his pastor to tell him that his marriage was in trouble. The pastor said, "I will drop everything I am doing and meet with you immediately."The man replied, "Oh, well I can't meet with you right now - I'm at work..." The pastor persisted, "Ok, well how about after you get off work?" The man said, "No, my son has a baseball game tonight." And on it went. You see the man wants to save his marriage as long as it is convenient. Now if that same man severely cut his hand he would find time to go to the hospital. If he wakes up desperately sick, he will find time to stay in bed and call the doctor. In fact, if a friend dies, he will find the time to attend the funeral. Truth is we do what we want to do, and find time for that which we believe is really vital. Only when seeking God is viewed as an urgent priority will we seek God with all our hearts.

There is a huge rivalry in college basketball between the University of Louisville and the University of Kentucky. The story is told that at one of the games between the two schools, an elderly woman was sitting alone with an empty seat next to her. Someone approached her and said, "Ma'am, I have rarely seen an empty seat in Rupp Arena, let alone at a game between these two teams. Whose seat is this?" The woman responded that she and her late husband had been season-ticket holders for 28 years, and the seat had belonged to him. He then asked, "Well, couldn't you find a friend or relative to come to the game with you?" She replied, "Are you kidding? They're all at my husband's funeral." When God becomes as much of a priority to us, as that woman's game was to her, we will make some progress.

We get alone with God for a *Purpose*.

To *Seek* Him. "that every one which sought the LORD" V.7

Not to get something *from* Him, but to get *to* Him.

But without faith *it is* impossible to please *him*: for he that comes to God must believe that he is, and *that* he is a rewarder of them that diligently seek him. Hebrews 11:6

To *Sense* His Presence. VV. 8-9

Today we do not have a pillar of fire but there is a definite manifestation of God's Presence.

He that has my commandments, and keeps them, he it is that loves me: and he that loves me shall be loved of my Father, and I will love him, and will manifest myself to him. John 14:21

Draw nigh to God, and he will draw nigh to you…" James 4:8

How does an omnipresent God draw near? It must be related to His manifested presence.

As one noted, "It is quite obvious that to Moses, praying for the manifested Presence of God was a consuming priority. To Moses having the Presence of God was as important to the spiritual future of Israel as having air to breathe was to their physical survival. Big issues demand a big response. For Moses, the Presence of God was the biggest issue imaginable."

To hear Him *Speak*. 9b-11

Today God does not speak to us through an audible voice, but the Holy Spirit speaking through the Written Word. We will not walk in the glory and set aside the Bible. Oh that the ultimate purpose of our lives would be to Seek God; Sense His Presence; and listen to Him Speak to us. When that purpose is set on the back burner our lives become stale and empty within. Earnest Hemingway traveled extensively as a big game hunter. He was married four times. A literary genius and yet confessed:

"I live in a vacuum that is as lonely as a radio tube when the batteries are dead, and there is no current to plug into."

Only God Himself can fill the void in our lives.

The *Premise*

We must be part of God's *Family.*

You have said I know you by name - that is true of every believer.

And this is life eternal, that they might know You the only true God, and Jesus Christ, whom You have sent. John 17:3

It is only when we have a personal life-changing encounter with Jesus Christ as our Savior that we can experience His Presence.

We must approach by God's *Favor.*

Moses had *found grace* - Grace is God's riches at Christ's expense. Even after we are saved we can only approach God based on the merit of Jesus Christ alone.

Jerry Bridges observes, "To say a person is morally bankrupt is to say he or she is completely devoid of any decent moral qualities. It's like comparing that person to Adolph Hitler. Now we are spiritually bankrupt. We owed a debt we could not pay. Then we learned salvation is a gift from God; it is entirely by grace through faith. We renounced confidence in any supposed righteousness of our own and turned in faith to Jesus Christ alone for our salvation. We essentially declared spiritual bankruptcy. Companies forced into bankruptcy have two options - Chapter 7 and Chapter 11. Chapter 11 deals with temporary bankruptcy. This means that given enough time we can work out our financial problems. But Chapter 7 is for a company that is finished. The question is, what kind of bankruptcy did we declare, when we were saved? We would say that it was a permanent spiritual bankruptcy. However, I think most of us live like it was a temporary bankruptcy. We recognize our best efforts cannot get us to heaven, but we do think that we can earn God's blessing in our daily lives. Nothing could be farther from reality!"

[8] For by grace are ye saved through faith; and that not of yourselves: *it is* the gift of God: [9] Not of works, lest any man should boast.
Ephesians 2:8-9

As ye have therefore received Christ Jesus the Lord, *so* walk you in him:
Colossians 2:6

Back in September 1994, Indian farmers in New Delhi, India protested the government's plan to import 3 million tons of Dutch dung to be used for farm fertilizer. Farmers knew there was no shortage of cows in India, so they took 6 ox carts piled high with top-quality, home-grown dung and dropped it off at the Parliament. Our merit and self-righteousness is nothing but dung in the eyes of God, and it matters little whether it is Baptist dung or Methodist dung or Charismatic dung!

⁸ Yes, all the things I once thought were so important are gone from my life. Compared to the high privilege of knowing Christ Jesus as my Master, firsthand, everything I once thought I had going for me is insignificant—dog dung. I've dumped it all in the trash so that I could embrace Christ Philippians 3:8 (MSG)

The *Prayer* 33:13

The *Petition*

For *Guidance - show me now Thy way* – this should be our constant petition.

⁶ The LORD executes righteousness and judgment for all that are oppressed. ⁷ He made known his ways unto Moses, his acts unto the children of Israel. Psalm 103:6-7

⁴ Show me thy ways, O LORD; teach me thy paths... ⁹ The meek will he guide in judgment: and the meek will he teach his way. Psalm 25:4, 9

¹¹ Teach me thy way, O LORD, and lead me in a plain path, because of mine enemies. Psalm 27:11

First, we are unable to discover God's way for ourselves. Second, only God Himself can show us His way. Third, it is as God condescends to show us His way that we get to know Him better."

23 O LORD, I know that the way of man *is* not in himself: *it is* not in man that walks to direct his steps. Jeremiah 10:23

For *God - that I may know Thee* .

This is the word used for sexual intimacy between a husband and a wife. It speaks of a heart that beats to know more of the God that we have come to know.

10 That I may know him, and the power of his resurrection, and the fellowship of his sufferings, being made conformable unto his death; Philippians 3:10

"We hunger to know God directly, not just to know facts about Him. In reality the need to know God does not allow us to dispense with knowing about God. Facts are essential to knowing any person. Sometimes love does seem to soar above words, but it always returns. The two ways of relating are not at odds with each other; they reinforce each other."

For *Grace - that I may find grace in Thy sight*

And of his fulness have all we received, and grace for grace. John 1:16

"We need one kind of grace in the days of prosperity and another in the days of adversity. We need one grace in the sunlit days of youth, and another when the shadows of age begin to lengthen. We need one grace when we feel that we are on top of things, and another when we are depressed and discouraged and near to despair. The grace of God is never static but always a dynamic thing. It never fails to meet the situation."

[9] Each time he said, "My grace is all you need. My power works best in weakness." So now I am glad to boast about my weaknesses, so that the power of Christ can work through me. [10] That's why I take pleasure in my weaknesses, and in the insults,

hardships, persecutions, and troubles that I suffer for Christ. For when I am weak, then I am strong.
2 Corinthians 12:9-10

The *Intercession* 13b

We must not merely pray for ourselves but also for others...

The *Promise* 14-16

Rest - My Presence shall go with thee.

10 Don't be afraid, for I am with you. Don't be discouraged, for I am your God. I will strengthen you and help you. I will hold you up with my victorious right hand. Isaiah 41:10

7 Be still in the presence of the LORD, and wait patiently for him to act. Don't worry about evil people who prosper or fret about their wicked schemes.
Psalm 37:7

28 Come unto me, all *you* that labour and are heavy laden, and I will give you rest. 29 Take my yoke upon you, and learn of me; for I am meek and lowly in heart: and ye shall find rest unto your souls. 30 For my yoke *is*

easy, and my burden is light. Matthew 11:28-30

Resolve - if Thy presence go not with me, carry us not from hence, where was "hence?"

A barren desert! Where were they going? To a Land flowing with milk and honey. Moses would rather stay in a barren desert with the manifested Presence of God, then go to a land flowing with blessing but without the manifested Presence of God. God being Omnipresent would, of course, be there, but that is a far cry from experiencing the manifested Presence of God. Nothing is worse than Jacob's cry, "God was in this place and I did not know it."

Result - a testimony!

"The Presence of God is the only thing that distinguishes God's people from all other peoples upon the face of the earth. We often give ourselves to clever designs and careful manipulations in order to gain distinctions above others.

Is it to be for possessions, human power, popularity, achievements that we are known among others? No, our one distinguishing characteristic must be the Presence of God in our lives."

The *Priority*

Is God really the priority of our lives?

Douglas Coupland writes, "Now - here is my secret: I tell it to you with an openness of heart that I doubt I shall ever achieve again, so I pray that you are in a quiet room as you hear these words. My secret is that I need God - that I am sick and can no longer make it alone. I need God to help me give, because I no longer seem to be capable of giving; to help me be kind, as I no longer seem capable of kindness; to help me love, as I seem beyond being able to love."

That is the secret of life in a nutshell - a realization of our need for God. A Daily Check list to experiencing the Manifested Presence of God:

Do I have any Thought of merit outside of the merit of Jesus Christ? Lu. 18:9-14

Do I Tolerate any known sin?

13 So roll up your sleeves, put your mind in gear, be totally ready to receive the gift that's coming when Jesus arrives. 14 Don't lazily slip back into those old grooves of evil, doing just what you feel like doing. You didn't know any better then; you do now. 15 As obedient children, let yourselves be pulled into a way of life shaped by God's life, a life energetic and blazing with holiness. 16 God said, "I am holy; you be holy." 1 Peter 1:13-16 (MSG)

What do we do with known sin? Admit it, Quit it and Forget it!

If we confess our sins, he is faithful and just to forgive us *our* sins, and to cleanse us from all unrighteousness. 1 John 1:9 Am I by the Holy Spirit rendering Total obedience to God? Jn. 14:21

Do I Talk to Him all the time? 1 Thess. 5:17

Do I Take God at His Word? 1 Cor. 3:16

Do I Travail in prayer? 2 Cor. 10:3-6

We must Treasure God's Word.

The word of Christ, let it be continually at home in you in abundance; with every wisdom teaching and admonishing each other by means of psalms, hymns, spiritual songs, with the grace singing in your hearts to God. Col. 3:16 Wuest

Trust God even in the dark.

10 Who *is* among you that fears the LORD, that obeys the voice of his servant, that walks *in* darkness, and hath no light? let him trust in the name of the LORD, and stay upon his God. 11 Behold, all ye that kindle a fire, that compass *yourselves* about with sparks: walk in the light of your fire, and in the sparks *that* you have kindled. This shall you have of mine hand; you shall lie down in sorrow.   Isaiah 50:10-11

Here is a person who has Reverence [fears] and Obedience [obeys] and yet walks in Darkness! Sometimes God Hides His manifested Presence. In those times, we must:

Keep *Living* for God. [walks...in darkness]

Lean on Him.

Do not *Light* your own fire!

Do not *Lecture* God on what to do.

[8] The wind blows where it wants, and you hear the sound thereof, but cannot tell whence it comes, and where it goes: so is every one that is born of the Spirit. John 3:8

The Holy Spirit is like the wind - speaking of:

a. His *Sovereignty* - The wind blows where it wills. Just as we do not tell the wind where and when to blow, we do not tell God what to do!

b. The wind has *Secrecy* - you cannot tell where it came from nor where it is going. We cannot figure out God either!

c. The winds *Sound* - you can tell when the wind is blowing and you can tell when it is not.

Our part is to set our sails; keep our sails washed in the blood; and prayerfully wait on Him.

Think in humility.

For thus says the high and lofty One that inhabits eternity, whose name *is* Holy; I dwell in the high and holy *place*, with him also *that is* of a contrite and humble spirit, to revive the spirit of the humble, and to revive the heart of the contrite ones.
Isaiah 57:15

Bro Lawrence, "We ought to surrender all things to God, seeking our only joy in Jesus. It matters very little whether He leads us through pain or pleasure - for both are the same to the soul that is truly committed to God's will. Oh, that we may be thrilled to even put on a watch for the glory of God. Let us cultivate the habit of talking with God every moment of every day, looking to Him for guidance and goodness and grace. Sure we get sidetracked and preoccupied with lesser things - but when our insensitivity is realized, we simply refocus our attention on Him. Prayer times are wonderful but no different from any other time, since we have made it our determination to lift our heart upward at all times. We must guard our thoughts, refusing to put our gaze on the useless and rejecting foolish fancies or prideful self exaltation. We have a business to run, the business of delighting ourselves in the Lord. We must come to grip with the truth that we have an inward rebellious nature that needs to be subdued and must have adversity often to drive us to deeper dependency upon God."

Chapter Four

STRENGTH FOR BATTLING THE *PRINCE* OF DARKNESS

[10] Finally, my brethren, be strong in the Lord, and in the power of his

might. ¹¹ Put on the whole armour of God, that ye may be able to stand against the wiles of the devil. ¹² For we wrestle not against flesh and blood, but against principalities, against powers, against the rulers of the darkness of this world, against spiritual wickedness in high *places*. ¹³ Wherefore take unto you the whole armour of God, that ye may be able to withstand in the evil day, and having done all, to stand. ¹⁴ Stand therefore, having your loins girt about with truth, and having on the breastplate of righteousness; ¹⁵ And your feet shod with the preparation of the gospel of peace; ¹⁶ Above all, taking the shield of faith, wherewith ye shall be able to quench all the fiery darts of the wicked. ¹⁷ And take the helmet of salvation, and the sword of the Spirit, which is the word of God: ¹⁸ Praying always with all prayer and supplication in the Spirit, and watching thereunto with all perseverance and supplication for all saints; Ephesians 6:10-18

By Divine Strengthening.

The *Source* of our strength.

Finally, my brethren, be strong – a present tense; imperative mood; in the passive voice. It is a command, to continually be strengthened by God. Our power does not come from ourselves but from an external source – God!

The *Sphere* of our strength.

in the Lord – our strength comes from the sphere of our union with Christ. A fish is a fascinating creature; it can dart about with great speed. It is strong, clean, and majestic. But there is one simple condition to its well-being and beauty – water! Take a fish out of water and it will immediately become helpless, dirty, and just plain ugly as it flops about gasping for air. Truth is, we have only one condition for our well-being and beauty it is abiding "In Christ." It is our union with Christ that gives us the only sphere of strength we have.

The *Supernatural* strengthening.

and in the power of His might – and is best translated, "that is" further explaining this power. It is His might not ours, the very power of God is available! It is not that He makes us strong, but that He becomes our strength (2 Cor. 12:9).

So we have strength for that comes from the Trinity. God the Father (Jer. 32:17); God the Son (Phil. 4:13); and God the Spirit (Ac. 1:8).

Strength for standing against temptation (1 Cor. 10:13), for preaching (1 Cor. 2:4-5), for witnessing (Ac. 1:8), etc.

By *Defensive Standing*

The *Repetition* – of the word "stand" vv. 11, 13, 14.

The needed *Recognition* - the focus is on the defensive not the offensive, just the opposite of looking for a demon behind every bush! The idea of standing is to "hold one's ground." We are to hold fast our drawing upon God's strength; to hold fast an awareness of our union with Christ; hold fast to positional truth:

Deeply loved no matter what because of Propitiation;

Completely forgiven and fully pleasing because of Justification;

Totally accepted because of Reconciliation;

Entirely a new person because of Regeneration;

Adequately empowered because of the indwelling Spirit;

You can add many things to this list...

I also like to think of standing related to our Identity with Christ (Gal. 2:20); or Ministry (1 Cor. 15:58), and related to our Intimacy (Hab. 4:17-19).

By *Devilish Struggling*

Against *Wiles* of the *Devil* – the word means "strategy, schemes, methods." The plural suggests that he has many different schemes. Devil = slanderer.

[8] Be sober, be vigilant; because your adversary the devil, as a roaring lion, walketh about, seeking whom he may devour: [9] Whom resist stedfast in the faith, knowing that the same afflictions

are accomplished in your brethren that are in the world. 1 Peter 5:8-9

I love those old 'B' Western movies. There was one with a Cowboy who would go into town with a huge rattlesnake in a glass jar. He would wager that no one could keep their hand on that jar, as that snake struck at him. One after another would pull his hand back, and that cowboy was becoming rich on their unbelief. Satan cannot stop one who refuses to be intimidated by Satan and his schemes. He is defeated through the blood of Christ.

Against *Wrestling* against the *Demonic*

Against demonic *Authority*

For we do not wrestle against flesh and blood, but against principalities- the source is not human but demonic! The word principalities is *archē* meaning, "Beginning, origin, authority, rule, domain, sphere of influence." It is translated "beginning" some 40 times. We have to struggle against these demons at the beginning of their interference. The Principle is we need to fight demons at the source of their attack which is "Looking." The Process is always the same: First Looking; then desiring; and finally taking (Gen. 3:6; 6:2/Josh. 7:21/2 Sam. 11:2-5).

We must resist these principalities at the beginning of their getting authority in our minds. A fish is wiser to shun the bait than try to get off once he has been hooked!

Against demonic *Ability*

against powers – we are not dealing with natural powers but supernatural opponents. We cannot struggle against supernatural powers with natural means. Power here is better translated "Authority." They seek authority, a place, a stronghold in our minds. The only way to have authority over demons is to be *under* the authority of Jesus Christ.

[7] Submit yourselves therefore to God. Resist the devil, and he will flee from you. James 4:7

Against the demonic *Inability* to be seen

against the rulers of the darkness of this world – darkness is the inability to see. Demons work hard at keeping us from seeing the invisible God and living life with eternity in mind. They do not want us to know, or take seriously the reality of their presence.

Against demonic *Impurity*

against spiritual wickedness in high places – demons are vile, nasty, sinful beings and want us to be such in our experience. They seek to get us to commit a particular sin over and over again, thus establishing a demonic stronghold. Our battle is not with people but demonic opposition that we have to deal with to preach effectively.

Back in 1665 there was a great plague in London, England. The Black Plague that killed thousands of people. People thought the problem was that they were breathing bad air. Doctors carried pockets full of roses and poises thinking it would help. Some doctors blew ashes in people's faces seeking to get them to sneeze, believing it would clear out their lungs.

Ring around the Roses,

Pocket full of Posies;

Ashes, Ashes, we all fall down!

The problem was they were fighting the wrong enemy! They didn't know about invisible germs, we have the same problem today many fail to recognize our invisible enemy.

By a *Decisive Suiting up*

Reality – "belt of truth." Satan works through lies, our defense is the Reality of God's truth.

JESUS IS OUR TRUTH! Jn.14:6

Conformity – "breastplate of righteousness" Satan works through sin, our defense is Imputed Righteousness from Jesus
and *Imparted* from the Holy Spirit.

JESUS IS OUR RIGHTEOUSNESS! 2 Cor. 5:21

Tranquility – [15] And your feet shod with the preparation of the gospel of peace; Satan seeks to work through fear, panic, and disturbing our trust in

God, our defense is to trust that God is Sovereignly on His throne.

JESUS IS OUR PEACE! Eph. 2:14

Dependency – "shield of faith." Satan works through doubt, our defense is an unwavering trust in His Person and Promises. Rom. 4:20-21

JESUS IS OUR FAITH! Heb. 12:2

Mentality – "helmet of salvation." Satan works through messing up our mind, our defense is to keep our mind on Christ and to live this life with eternity in mind.

JESUS IS OUR FOCUS. Heb. 12:2

Authority – "Sword of the Spirit." Satan works through personal opinion, but our defense is the Word of God. 2 Tim. 3:16-17

JESUS IS THE WORD! Jn. 1:1

The *Shelling* of the enemy

Prayer is *Surprisingly Depicted*

It is the greater *Work (*Jn. 14:12).

What are these greater works? Miracles? Hardly! Do we know of any believer who is raising the dead, walking on water, or feeding the multitude with a boy's lunch? So what are these works that are greater than what the Lord did? It begins with a conjunction, "and" which of course is a connector. It is only complete as we consider what it is connected to. If we read vv. 12-13 together, he is saying that the greater works of verse 12 are accomplished by none other than prayer! It is so startling that He has to repeat in verse 14.

The idea is that just as Jesus did nothing of Himself, but only what the Father did through Him, so we are to do nothing of ourselves but by God's Spirit working through us and that by prayer.

It is by prayer that we are engaged in the *Warfare.*

Here we stand will all of this wonderful armor on us – now what? Where is this battlefield and how do we engage in it? It is by way of prayer. It is prayer which pulls down the satanic strongholds (2 Cor. 10:3-6) and zeroing in on the enemy. Prayer is the place where the battle is won or lost.

It is often *Strangely Denied*

I think prayer is one of the most mysterious things on the planet. Often we see little correlation between our prayers and things actually happening in our lives or the lives of others. My favorite evangelist is Billy Graham, of course not counting my friend Sam Moore, I was a counselor in a Billy Graham crusade way back in 1975, and it was called *Euro-fest* and took place in Brussels, Belgium. I can tell you much prayer went into those crusades. During a crusade in Washington D.C., back in 1952 they prayed that the rain would stop and it did. Billy then told the crowd, "I believe God does intervene. I also believe God did intervene today, as He has in days gone by when we have prayed concerning the matter of the weather." Then with a smile, and his belt of truth firmly on, said, "But in all fairness, I have to remember that we prayed once out in Portland, Oregon, and it poured down!"

Like it or not, deny it if you will, but we all have those Portland, Oregon experiences that we cannot explain or understand.

Prayer can be *Supernaturally Delayed*

All we have to do is read the tenth chapter of the book of Daniel. There the godly man Daniel prayed, and his prayers were hindered for some twenty-one days! It was hindered by demonic opposition. I have had more than one prayer hindered, and a whole lot longer than twenty-one days!

Prayer is *Simply Described*

Prayer is to be *Total*

With all prayer and petition - prayer needs to be balanced, it is not all praise or all asking but all kinds of different prayers are need.

Prayer is to be *Perpetual*

pray at all times – there is never an hour of the day where we do not need to be prayerful because Satan takes no holidays, vacations or days off. See Lu. 18:1/1 Thess. 5:17.

Prayer is to be *Supernatural.*

in the Spirit – just as Jesus did nothing on his own during the incarnation neither can we (Jude 20/Rom. 8:26). He must both initiate and maintain our prayer lives.

Prayer should be *Watchful.*

and with this in view, be on the alert – Mt. 26:41.

Prayer is to be *Universal*

with all perseverance and petition for all the saints – we are not to pray just for those we like but it is to be for all the saints. I have made it a habit to pray for all of my members, by name, on a daily basis.

Prayer is to be Personal.

and pray on my behalf, that utterance may be given to me in the opening of my mouth, to make known with boldness the mystery of the gospel, [20] *for which I am an ambassador in chains; that in proclaiming it I may speak boldly, as I ought to speak –* Paul made specific prayer requests, so should we.

During the Gulf War they were very concerned about the release of biological weapons. Gen. Krulak recalls that American forces began an attack from the southwest, on Feb. 21, 1991 at 4 in the morning. Now the prevailing winds in the Gulf area blow from the northeast to the southwest. Thus if chemicals are released it will blow right into the direction of these troops. It was such a concern that the General petitioned many to pray about it. The word got out of the need, both there and back home.

Only hours before they moved out the winds shifted to blow from the southeast to the northeast thus if biological weapons were used it would blow back in the enemies face. Those winds blew in that direction for four days and within 30 minutes of the surrender, the winds shifted back.

Con:

We cannot study the Scriptures unless we deal with Satan and His demonic forces.

A mighty fortress is our God,
a bulwark never failing;
our helper he amid the flood
of mortal ills prevailing.
For still our ancient foe
doth seek to work us woe;
his craft and power are great,
and armed with cruel hate,
on earth is not his equal.

Did we in our own strength confide,
our striving would be losing,
were not the right man on our side,
the man of God's own choosing.
Dost ask who that may be?
Christ Jesus, it is he;
Lord Sabaoth, his name,
from age to age the same,
and he must win the battle.

Chapter Five

STUDYING FOR THE STUDY

PART ONE

The Perfect Pastor – He has one brown eye and one blue eye; He visits all day long but never leaves his place of study; He is 65 years old, and will be 30 on his next birthday; he loves and ministers to the young people and spends all his time with the elderly; He preaches long and hard, but he is always finished within 15 minutes.
We cannot be perfect pastors, but we can be good Bible teachers. We can work at being good Bible teachers, here are a few helpful things for us to consider in that endeavor.

Realization what we study comes from God.

The following is a chart that overviews how the Bible came from God, fill in the blanks: God – Revelation –Human Authors –Inspiration –Original Autographs –Collection -66 books – Copying –Manuscripts – English – Illumination – the believer being under authority.

Let's do a quick overview:

MIRACLE OF THE BIBLE:

Written over a period of a 1,500-year span. Moses wrote the first book of the Bible, Genesis about 1400 B.C., and the apostle John the last book, Revelation, about 96 A.D.

Written by some 40 authors, from every walk of life:

Moses, a political leader, trained in the universities of Egypt.

Peter, a fisherman.

Amos, a herdsman.

Joshua, a military General.

Nehemiah, a cupbearer.

Daniel, a Prime Minister.

Luke, a Doctor.

Solomon, a King.

Matthew, a tax collector.

Paul a former Rabbi.

Just to name a few...

Written in different places:

Moses in the wilderness.

Jeremiah in a dungeon.

Daniel on a hillside and Palace.

Paul in prison

John in exile on Patmos

Etc.

Written at different times: both in times of peace and war.

Written in three languages: Hebrew, the major portion of the Old Testament; Aramaic, in Ezra 4:8-6:18; 7:12-26/ Dan.2:4-7:28/ Jer. 10:11; and Greek in the New Testament.

The miracle is that even though the Bible was written over a large period of time by men who did not know each other, and had very little in common, there is a definite unity of mind from Genesis to Revelation! There are no discrepancies, contradictions, or disagreements when all the facts are known. That makes this a miracle Book.

THE MECHANICS OF THE BIBLE:

Bible – the English word Bible is derived from the Greek word *biblion*, which means "book" or "roll." The name comes from *Byblos,* which denotes the papyrus plant that grew in marshes or river banks, primarily along the Nile River. Writing materials were made from papyrus plants. Eventually, the plural form *biblia* was used by Latin speaking Christians to denote all the books of the Old and New Testament (Dan. 9:2).

Scripture – the Greek word is *graphe,* which means "writing." In the Old Testament, this writing was recognized as carrying great authority (2 Kings 14:6/ 2 Chronicles 23:18/Ezra 3:2/Nehemiah 10:34). The writings of the Old Testament were eventually collected into three groups called the Law; Prophets; and Writings and consisted of the 39 books of our Old Testament (Lu. 24:44).

In the New Testament, the Greek verb *grapho* is used about 90 times in reference to the Bible, while the noun form *graphe* is used 51 times, almost exclusively of Holy Scriptures. The term the Scriptures designates collectively all the parts of the Scripture (Matthew 21:42; 22:29; 26:54/Luke 24:27, 32, 45/John 5:39/Romans 15:4/2 Peter 3:16) or individual parts of the Scripture (Mark 12:10; 15:28/John 13:18; 19:24, 36/Acts 1:16; 8:35/Romans 11:2/2 Timothy 3:16). The phrase The Scripture says, is a synonym for quoting God Himself (Romans 4:3; 9:17; 10:11/Galatians 4:3/I Timothy 5:18). 2 Timothy 3:16 declares that all the Scriptures are God breathed, inspired by God (2 Peter 3:16).

Old and New Testament – the Hebrew word for testament is *berith* meaning Covenant or agreement. The Greek word is *diatheke* and means covenant. The Old Covenant is preparation for Jesus' coming, the Law showed man was a sinner, the animal sacrifices showed how God would forgive sin through His perfect substitute, the Lord Jesus Christ (John 1:29). The New Covenant is the fulfillment of the Old Covenant.

THE MESSAGE OF THE BIBLE:

The Lord Jesus Christ (Luke 24:27/John 5:39, 46/Acts 26:22-23; 28:23).

There are also many other themes: sin; redemption; kingdom; faith; etc.

The Kingdom of God is a very important theme in helping us understand our Bible:

In the Old Testament the Kingdom is *Promised*; in the Gospels it is *Proclaimed* and rejected; in the New Testament epistles it is *Postponed*; and in the book of Revelation it is *Presented.*

I also believe it is impossible to understand the need for a future earthly kingdom without understanding the importance of the Abrahamic Covenant as the foundation for all proceeding covenants and how this covenant has not yet been totally fulfilled.

| Palestinian Cov. | New Cov. | Davidic Cov. |

(Dt.30)	(Jer. 31)	(2 Sam.7)
Land	Seed	Blessing

Abrahamic Covenant Foundation which promised a land, seed, and a blessing.

MANY WAYS TO ORGANIZE THE BIBLE:

If we organized it in book shelf form:

History section: Law of Moses - Genesis; Exodus; Leviticus; Numbers; Deuteronomy. Joshua; Judges; Ruth; 1 & 2 Samuel; 1& 2 Kings; 1 & 2 Chronicles; Ezra; Nehemiah.

Poetry: Job; Psalms; Proverbs; Ecclesiastes; Song of Solomon.

Prophecy: Major Prophets - Isaiah; Jeremiah; Lamentations; Ezekiel; Minor Prophets -Daniel; Hosea; Joel; Amos; Obadiah; Jonah; Micah; Nahum; Habakkuk; Zechariah; Malachi.

Biography: Matthew; Mark; Luke; John.

History: Acts

Paul's Letters: Romans; 1 & 2 Corinthians; Galatians; Ephesians; Philippians; Colossians; 1 & 2 Thessalonians; 1 & 2 Timothy; Titus; Philemon.

Other Letters: Hebrews; James; 1 & 2 Peter; 1 & 2 & 3 John; Jude.

Prophecy: Revelation.

It is helpful to organize the whole thing in a time frame and in relationship to other books:

Job, for example was written during the time period of the book of Genesis…

Ruth, was written during the period of the book of Judges…

Psalms, was written during the period of 1 & 2 Samuel…

Esther, during the time of Ezra…

Therefore if you are studying the Psalms, it is helpful to know 1 & 2 Samuel for background material.

The book of Acts comes alive when you realize it in relationship to other books.

Early church growth, which takes place in Jerusalem and Judah are covered in Acts 1-12, during which time the book of James was written...

Paul's First Missionary Journey is found in Acts 13-14, in which the book of Galatians was written...

Paul's Second Missionary Journey, is depicted in Acts 16-18, both 1 & 2 Thessalonians was written then.

Paul's Third Missionary Journey found in Acts 19-21, during that time 1 & 2 Corinthians and Romans was written...

We have Paul's first Prison term, found in Acts 22-28, when Philemon; Colossians; Ephesians; and Philippians were written...

The book of Acts ends, but not Paul's life, he is released at which time 1 Timothy and Titus is written...

He has a second prison term, in which he is beheaded and his last letter is 2 Timothy.

Knowing this background is vital for understanding the background of the epistles.

You can get an overview of the Bible to help you get a handle on it:

Roots of the Nation of Israel, Genesis.

Redemption of the Nation, Exodus.

Requirements for the Nation, Leviticus.

Refusal of the Nation, Numbers.

Reminder to the Nation, Deuteronomy.

Reception of the Nation, Joshua.

Rebellion of the Nation, Judges.

Remnant of the Nation, Ruth.

Rulers of the Nation, 1 Sam-2 Kings.

Retrospection in 1 & 2 Chronicles.

Restoration in Ezra.

Reconstruction in Nehemiah.

Remnant that did not return to Jerusalem in Esther.

Rhythm of the Nation – Job about *Suffering;* Psalms abut *Singing*; Proverbs about *Sayings*; Ecclesiastes about *Searching*; Song of Solomon about *Sharing.*

Revealers of God's Word – Pre-exilic Prophets : Joel; Jonah; Amos; Hosea; Micah; Isaiah; Nahum; Zephaniah; Habakkuk; Jeremiah. Exilic Prophets: Daniel; Ezekiel; Obadiah. Post-exilic Prophets: Haggai; Zechariah; and Malachi.

John Phillips has a good summary of New Testament:

The Christian and his Beliefs:

The Fundamental – Matthew/Mark/Luke/John/ Romans.

The False – Galatians/Colossians/Hebrews/2 Corinthians/2 Timothy/

2 Peter/Jude.

The Future – 1 Thessalonians/2 Thessalonians/Revelation.

The Christian and his Brethren.

The Origins of the Church – Acts.

The Operation of the Church – 1 Corinthians/Ephesians.

The Officers of the Church – 1 Timothy/ Titus.

The Christian and his Behavior.

Dealing with Situations – Philippians.

With Slavery – Philemon.

With Sincerity – James.

With Suffering – 1 Peter.

With Sonship – 1 John.

With Separation – 2 John.

With Strife – 3 John.

Anyway we need to realize that the Bible comes from God.
God Revealed His Word to the authors of the Bible and enabled them to write those words down; and then by His Sovereign power preserved them for us today. This Bible is therefore from God and is our authority; our boss; our

Control Tower. We flew here from Rogers, AR. To do that, the pilot needed to be under the authority of the control tower. The pilot had a limited vantage point. He could not see underneath or above the airplane. Even with all of their instruments, they cannot see all the weather conditions that they will encounter during their flight. The folks in the control tower provide pilots with help, direction, and guidance that they will need. The Word of God is the control tower for the Christian. Where we have only a limited vantage point, God's Word can communicate to us what we would not know by ourselves.

We must believe that the Bible is from God and is our authority! If the Bible teaches a doctrine then we teach that doctrine; if the Bible commands something then we are to obey those commands; we have all played Simon says! We need to learn to play the Bible says.

There is a game show in my country called, *Who Wants to Be a Millionaire?* People are asked questions and if they give the right answers they can become rich. If you do not know the answer you are given what they call "lifelines." That means they can call a *friend* and ask them what is the answer to the question; or they can ask the *audience* to help and go with what the majority have to say. In life we have one reliable lifeline – it is not what we think or what friends think or what the majority thinks – our lifeline is the Bible! It tells us what God has to say! What's our lifeline? Is it our personal opinion, preferences or feeling? It must be God's Word!

Illumination must also come from God.

⁹ But as it is written, Eye has not seen, nor ear heard, neither have entered into the heart of man, the things which God hath prepared for them that love him. ¹⁰ But God has revealed *them* unto us by his Spirit: for the Spirit searches all things, yea, the deep things of God. ¹¹ For what man knows the things of a man, save the spirit of man which is in him? even so the things of God knows no man,

but the Spirit of God. ¹² Now we have received, not the spirit of the world, but the spirit which is of God; that we might know the things that are freely given to us of God. 1 Corinthians 2:9-12

⁷ That is why the Holy Spirit says, "Today when you hear his voice, ⁸ don't harden your hearts as Israel did when they rebelled, when they tested me in the wilderness. Hebrews 3:7-8

The Holy Spirit is the *Source* of the Scriptures

¹⁶ All scripture *is* given by inspiration of God, and *is* profitable for doctrine, for reproof, for correction, for instruction in righteousness: ¹⁷ That the man of God may be perfect, thoroughly furnished unto all good works. 2 Timothy 3:16-17

The Holy Spirit also allows us to make *Sense* out of the Bible

¹³ When the Spirit of truth comes, he will guide you into all truth. He will not speak on his own but will tell you what

he has heard. He will tell you about the future. ¹⁴ He will bring me glory by telling you whatever he receives from me. ¹⁵ All that belongs to the Father is mine; this is why I said, 'The Spirit will tell you whatever he receives from me.' John 16:13-15

I wear these glasses because without them I cannot read the Bible. The older I get, it seems that the print of my Bible is getting smaller. I have to squint in order to see. But when I put these glasses on, I can read the Bible with ease. The Holy Spirit is like these glasses. He allows us to see what the Bible really means.

The Holy Spirit will only help us if we are willing to *Submit* to what we read.

If any man will do his will, he shall know of the doctrine, whether it be of God, or *whether* I speak of myself. John 7:17

You will never be able to eat solid spiritual food and understand the deeper things of God's Word until you become better Christians and learn right from wrong by practicing doing right. Hebrews 5:14 (TLB)

Anne Sullivan, who tutored Helen Keller who was deaf, dumb, and blind, said, "I saw clearly that it was useless to try to teach her language or anything else until she learned to obey me. I have thought about it a great deal, and the more I think, the more certain I am that obedience is the gateway through which knowledge comes."

Prayer is needed

We must pray before, during, and after we study the Bible.

Open thou mine eyes, that I may behold wondrous things out of thy law. Psalm 119:18

A few years ago, my son and his wife were *expecting* a baby. When a woman is pregnant we say, "She is expecting." Prayer keeps us in an attitude of expecting – we are expecting God to speak to us through His Word, we are expecting Him to give birth to a sermon! Prayer keeps us in touch with God, and keeps our hearts open to God.

Observation is our part.

Observation by *Reflecting*, we need to pay attention to what the Bible is actually saying.

Sir William Osler was a physician. He was always trying to impress upon his students the importance of observation. Once he held up a bottle which contained a urine sample. He told the students that sometimes it is possible by testing to determine what disease a patient suffered. He then dipped a finger into the fluid and then into his mouth. He then passed out that bottle and told them to taste of that bottle *as he* had done. As the bottle was passed among the students, they reluctantly sampled the contents. When they were finished he said, "Gentlemen, now you can appreciate the importance of observation. If you would have been observant you would have noticed that I put my index finger into the bottle, but my middle finger into my mouth!"

Observation requires much *Reading.*

Let the Bible tell us what it is saying. We must not come to the Bible with our own ideas. We must be open to what it is saying, not what we want it to say. Many are like the old man who was hard of hearing. One day while they were sitting on the porch, his wife said to him, "I love you." He said, "What did you say?" She repeated, "I love you!" He looked with scorn and said, "Well, I'm tired of you too!"

Read it *Repeatedly*.

We simply cannot read it too much. When John G. Mitchell, of Multnomah School of the Bible, was pastor of the First Presbyterian Church in Tacoma, Washington, he heard Dr. G. Campbell Morgan preach. The man knew his text, and young Mitchell was impressed. In fact, he asked the visiting Bible teacher how he understood Scripture so well. "If I told you, you wouldn't do it," Morgan said. "Just try me," Mitchell insisted. The veteran preacher replied, "Before I study a book, I read it fifty times." Beloved, if you want to learn God's Word, then read and re-read the Bible repeatedly.

Therefore, observation requires *Reflecting and Reading.* We need to think, to meditate on God's Word (Josh.1:8/Psa. 1). Like a coffee percolator – the water goes up a small tube and drains down through the coffee grounds. It goes through this cycle until the coffee and water are one.

Read it *Discerningly*.

Discover the key word, the *main theme* - What one word would sum up the passage? Example, if we were studying the book of Jude. We would begin by reading it over and over again asking "What is the main thought of this book?" Notice how often the word "ungodly" is used – 6 times! vv. 4, 15, 18

Now since it is written to the godly about the ungodly we might have as our big idea: *How the Godly deal with the Ungodly.* As you work through the book, repeatedly ask the question, what is the one word, that might describe the passage.

Therefore, as we read Jude 1-2, and ask what is the one word that would describe the passage. It is clearly a greeting.

[1] Jude, the servant of Jesus Christ, and brother of James, to them that are sanctified by God the Father, and preserved in Jesus Christ, *and* called: [2] Mercy unto you, and peace, and love, be multiplied. Jude 1:1-2

Now in keeping with our basic theme that describes the book of Jude, we might describe these first two verses as: *A Descriptive greeting to the Godly, who have to deal with the ungodly.* We work through the book like that.

Next, we should make an outline of the entire book of Jude; this comes from reading and rereading.

Once you have your main theme, organize it in the form of an *outline.*

I..A *Descriptive* greeting to the Godly who have to deal with the Ungodly. 1-2

II. Divine *Direction* given to the Godly Jude about the Ungodly. 3-4

III. The *Demonstration* of judgment against the Ungodly. 5-7

IV. The *Depiction* of the Ungodly. 8-16

V. The *Defense* against the Ungodly. 17-23

VI. The *Doxology that* encourages the Godly as they struggle against the Ungodly. 24-25

Then we go back to our first point:

I. A *Descriptive* greeting to the Godly who have to deal with the Ungodly. 1-2

Next we repeat the process of reading, discovering our basic word and then outlining it.

Sub: A Descriptive greeting to the Godly, who have to deal with the ungodly.

Outline:

I...The Godly Author. 1:1

The author's *Identity - Jude*

The author's *Mercy* - not Judas Iscariot

The author's *Slavery - a servant*

The author's *Christology - of Jesus Christ*

The author's Humility - *and brother of James*

Sub: The privileges of the godly.

Outline:

II. The Godly Audience. 1:2

A. Called by God's Spirit [assumed] – called.

B. Sanctified by God the Father – sanctified by

C. Preserved in Jesus Christ - *preserved*

Sub: The prayer for these godly believers.

Outline:

1. The Multiplication.

2. The Manifestation.

a. Of Mercy.

b. Of Peace.

c..Of Love.

Now, we just slowly *work through the passage, getting a subject and an outline.*

That is enough to digest for now – we begin by realizing that (1) our Bible comes from God; (2) Only the Holy Spirit can help us to understand; (3) Pray all the time; (4) Discover what one word sums up the passage and outline it. All we need to get started is a real hunger for God and a desire for God to speak to us by His Spirit through His Word. I am not saying my way is the only way or even the best way, but as Willie Nelson sings, "The night life, ain't no good life, but it's my life." This is the way I do it! I had someone the other day tell me he did not like the way I preach, I always go through a Book of the Bible verse-by-verse. I said, well brother that's alright, find a way that works for you and glorifies God. There was an old man who was known for walking with God and teaching His Word. A young man wanted to know God and His word like that, so he went to the old man who was mediating on God's word by a river. He asked him how he could know God and His word in such an intimate way. The old man grabbed the young man by the back of his neck and thrust him into the river. The young man struggled for air. Finally he let him up and said, "When you want to know God and His Word, like you wanted that breath of air…you'll find the secret to knowing God through His Word. Hunger is more important then method…

PART TWO

Kathleen Norris and her husband were visiting a man named Arlo. He was a rugged, self-made man who was facing terminal cancer. During their visit, Arlo told about his grandfather, a Christian who gave him and his wife an expensive leather Bible with their names printed in gold lettering. Arlo left it in the box and never opened it. But for months afterwards his grandfather kept asking if he liked the Bible. Finally, Arlo grew curious enough to open the Bible. He found that his grandfather had placed a twenty-dollar bill in front of every book of that Bible. One before each book of the Bible. Many are like Arlo, they do not know how valuable the Bible is because they never really open it and study it. We have looked at the need to realize the (1) Bible comes from God; (2) Only the Holy Spirit can give us understanding of it; (3) we need to pray all the time; (4) we need to discover one word that will sum up the passage we are studying and then outline it. Now after Observation comes interpretation.

Interpretation

Context

The Context of what goes before and what comes after the passage we are studying. For example if you take Phil.

2:12, without the context you will misunderstand what it is saying.

¹² Wherefore, my beloved, as you have always obeyed, not as in my presence only, but now much more in my absence, work out your own salvation with fear and trembling. Philippians 2:12

This has been used to teach that we have to work *for* our salvation or in order to stay saved. Which would contradict many passages of Scripture, like Eph. 2:8-9, for example. But the next verse or the context explains, "It is God who works..." We can only work *out* what God has *already* worked in and that work is a work of God.

The overall context or what dispensation is the passage found in? Everybody is a dispensationalist of some sort – nobody here this morning is naked like Adam and Eve in the dispensation of innocence; nobody brought a lamb to sacrifice; and no one of sound mind confesses that there is no more sickness as we will see in the future Kingdom. We may disagree as to how many dispensations but not to the fact that there are different dispensations. A dispensation is related to the different ways that God relates to mankind. Like different *administrations* among various presidents.

Overall view of Dispensations:

Innocence – Gen. 1:26-3:6

Conscience – 4:1-8:14

Human Government – Gen.8:15-11:32

Promise – Gen. 12:1-Ex.18:27

Law – Ex. 19:1-Ac.1:26

Church – Ac. 2-Rev. 4

Kingdom – Rev. 20:

Pattern for each Dispensation:

They begin with a new *Revelation*.

There is a *Requirement*.

There is a *Rejection* of that requirement.

There is therefore *Retribution*.

For more detail on this, get my book Ephesians: *A Manual for Survival,* a verse by verse study on the book of Ephesians.

Cross-references

The best commentary on the Bible – is the Bible! I recommend that you get a *Strong's Concordance*:

Look up the word in the Strong's concordance, which lists words alphabetically.

If the word is in the Bible it will be listed, take for example the word *predestinate*

Then below there are scriptures listed:

PREDESTINATE [2]

he also did p to be conformed to..............Rom.8:29   4309

Moreover whom he did p, them he............Rom. 8:30   4309

PREDESTINATED [2]

Having p us unto the adoption of............Eph. 1:5   4309

being p according to the
purpose............Eph. 1:11   4309

Now go to the back of the concordance and look up the number to the far right - 4309. Remember that if you are in the Old Testament you will be looking in the Old Testament Dictionary; and if you're in the New Testament you look under the New Testament Dictionary in the back.

4309 προπιζω [6 x] proorizo pro-or-id-zo; from 4253 and 3724; *to limit in advance*, i.e. (fig) *predetermine:* - determine before [1x], predestinate [4x]. This word denotes "to mark out beforehand, to determine before, foreordain"; (1) in Acts 4:28, "determine before"; (2) in Rom. 8:29-30 and Eph. 1:5, 11, "predestinate." See: TDNT - 5:456, 728; BAGD - 709b; THAYER - 541a. [The New Strong's Expanded Exhaustive Concordance of the Bible]

Warning: You have to consider the Context in order to understand the meaning of a word. Studying a word without considering the context is worthless. You can study the word *ice* for days and all you know is that it is "frozen water." But is it?

Somebody might be dealing in *ice*, a slang term for cocaine! In that context it has nothing to do with frozen water.

The mob might decide to *ice* someone, a slang to take that person's life.

One might be about to *ice* a cake – frosting!

An offended friend might be as cold as *ice*.

Take the word *trunk* – is it a tree trunk; a trunk in the attic; a trunk of a car; etc.

The meaning of words must be determined by the context. Take the word *lion* in the scriptures – only when you are talking about an animal, will studying the word be helpful. It can be a reference to *Babylon* (Jer. 4:7); or the nation of *Israel* (Ezk.19:2); or an analogy for Satan (1 Pet. 5:8); and even Jesus Christ Himself (Rev. 5:5).

Take the word *Run* – if you just study the word you might come up with the definition of walking fast. But the word is used of not only a man running, but of one's nose running; a washing machine running; running the pool table; leaving a faucet running, running for office; etc.

For example take the word *ekklēsía*; a called out assembly has to be identified by its context:

It can be referring to an assembly of Jewish people (Ac. 7:38).

It can refer to a pagan assembly (Ac. 19:32, 39, 41).

It can refer to the Body of Christ, which includes all believers from Pentecost to the Rapture (Col. 1:18).

It can refer to a local church (1 Cor. 1:2).

 That's probably enough for today. As you are beginning to see Bible Study involves a lot of work – it is not for the lazy. But it's worth it! I have had a guitar since I was a teenager. I have owned several guitars, and the one I have now is an Alvarez. It is an expensive guitar. However, after years of owning it – I still cannot play very well! Why? I am just too lazy to really play it. It may sit there in my closet for months without it ever being used. We can own a Bible for years and know very little about it. The problem, we are too lazy to really study.

PART THREE

Have you ever seen a straight river? Canals are straight, but all rivers seem to be crooked. We call it "meandering." Why are rivers crooked? Because the natural tendency of a river is to take the easiest way around any obstacle. So rivers are always crooked, and they always run downhill. When it comes to Bible study we cannot be like rivers. We must realize that it is not easy to really study the Bible, but that is what we are called to do. Last time we began to look at how to interpret the Bible; we looked at the need to see the Context and the value of Cross references... We now continue with how to interpret the Bible.

Cultural setting

Getting the overall Principle of a Passage:

Step 1.

Looking at the *original* situation. Question: What did the text mean to the biblical audience? Example read Josh. 1:1-9, and you discover that (a) Israel was about to enter the Promised Land; (b) Moses had just died and Joshua was entering a new leadership position; and (c) He received encouragement from God's Presence and verbal word.

Step 2.

Look for *Differences* between the original audience and us. Question: What are the differences between the biblical audience and us? We should see that (a) We are not Israel; (b) We are not living under the Old Covenant; (c) We are not entering the Promised Land; (d) We are not new leaders of a Nation.

Step 3.

Looking for *Similarities.* Question: What is the theological principle in this text? Try to identify any similarities between the situation of the biblical audience and our situation.

The principle should be reflected in the text.

The principle should be timeless and not tied to a specific situation.

The principle should not be culturally bound.

The principle should be relevant to both the biblical and the contemporary audience: (a) We are God's people; (b) We are in a Cov. relationship with God; (c) We may be entering some new leadership position; (d) We do need to claim God's promises; (e) We need God's presence to face our difficulties in life.

Step 4.

Question: How should individual Christians today apply the theological principle in their lives?"

[From, Grasping God's Word, Duvall and Hays, pp. 22-24]

Getting the Principle is vital to making the passage relevant. So when Paul commands "Be not drunk with wine, but be filled with the Spirit" (Eph. 5:18), we realize that the command is not limited to wine. The principle goes beyond wine; it would include things like any alcohol, drugs, etc.

Political culture:

Why did King Belshazzar offer the third position in the Babylonian kingdom to Daniel instead of the second position? History sources reveal that at that time Belshazzar was only second in command. His father Nabonidus was out of the country so the best he could offer Daniel was the third spot.

Religious culture:

Moses commanded "not to cook a young goat in its mother's milk." (Ex. 23:19; 34:26/Deut. 14:21) He did this because according to archeological discoveries it was a pagan ritual practiced by the Canaanites.

Economic culture:

Job 22:6 Eliphaz accused Job of having "taken pledges from you brother for no reason." The background is that if someone owed someone money they could not pay. The one owed the money could take the debtors coat as a pledge of future payments, but must return it at night so the person could use it as a blanket and keep warm. Truth is, Job was not guilty of doing this but was being falsely accused (31:19-22).

Legal culture:

In 2 Ki. 2:9 Elisha asked Elijah to give him a "double portion of his spirit." Was he power hungry? Was he asking for twice as much power? No, he was simply requesting to be his successor. The firstborn in a family was given a double share of his father's estate (Deut. 21:17).

Agricultural culture:

What would Amos call the women of Bethel "cows of Bashan?" These cows, located northeast of the Sea of Galilee, were known for having an easy life of grazing their way to fatness. The woman of Bethel had become wealthy and lazy! Amos 4:1

Clothing culture:

Why does the Bible mean when it tells us to "gird up the loins of our minds?" 1 Pet. 1:13 In that day when a man worked or ran or engaged in battle he tucked his robe into his sash so he could move freely.

Domestic culture:

What did the man in Lu. 9:59 mean by saying "let me go bury my father first?" It did not mean that his father had just died. The man felt obligated to take care of his father until he died, no doubt so he would get his father's inheritance. He was willing to put Jesus on the back burner for several years.

Geographical culture:

What is significant about the message to the Laodicean church being lukewarm, not hot or cold? He is comparing them to the water supply. Water was piped into Laodicea from

Heirapolis about 6 miles away. When the water left the hot springs in Heirapolis it was hot, but by the time it reached them it was lukewarm.

The bottom line is that understanding the culture is vital to understanding what the Bible is saying. For example, Mt. 17:24-27 seems extremely odd, I have been fishing for years and have never caught one with money in its mouth. The fish in the passage is a tilapia, a fish which actually carries its eggs in its mouth. If the young fish become frightened, they head for mother's mouth for protection. Often the mamma fish will pick up an object to prevent the babies from invading her mouth. That day by God's providential moving this fish picked up a shekel that was obviously on the bottom of the lake. There are various helps in explaining the cultural background. Many Commentaries give helpful insight; Today's Handbook of Bible Times & Customs; Harpers Encyclopedia of Bible Life; The New Manners and Customs of Bible times; etc.

Also, some cultural practices are temporary and others are still binding. When the Bible says greet one another with a holy kiss it is not still a normal thing. In our culture a warm handshake is comparable…

Trans: That is enough for today. Let's realize how important it is to understand what the Bible meant to those whom it was originally spoken. Where can you bridge the gap between the original audience and us? As a Good Bible Dictionary, I personally like the Holman Bible Dictionary. Have you ever watched a movie and missed the first five minutes of it? You don't know what's going on. That's how it is when we try to study the Bible without any knowledge of the culture of the Bible.

Always remember that knowing God's Word does not come by accident. We need to hear, read, study, memorize, and meditate upon God's Word. Just use your pinky for Hear, next finger for Read; next Study; next finger for Memorize; and your thumb for Meditation.

PART FOUR

National Review magazine took a survey of what high school students knew about the Bible. Here are some of the results of that survey:

Adam and Eve were created from an apple tree.

Noah's wife was called Joan of Ark.

Lot's wife was a pillar of salt by day and a ball of fire by night.

Moses died before he ever reached Canada and Joshua led the Hebrews in the battle of Geritol.

Solomon had 300 wives and 700 porcupines.

Samson was a strongman who slayed the Philistines with the ax of the apostles.

Obviously our young people don't know much about the Bible, but it's up to us to teach them. We are still looking at how to interpret the Bible. We have looked at Context, Cross-references, and Cultural setting. Now we continue.

One of the most important things we can do is to have a daily devotion or what is called a Quiet time; this is a pattern that might be helpful:

How to have a Quiet time:

1. Make it a *Priority* – a firm decision to set aside a time daily to seek God.

2. Have a specific *Place* – a room, a chair, a place of solitude.

3. Have a *Plan* – same time, same place, every single day.

4. Bring some *Paper* – a notebook to write down thoughts, impressons, insights, promises, etc.

5. Have a *Program:*

Singing – get a small hymbook and sing outloud to the Lord.

Scripture:

Any examples to follow…

Any exhortations…

Any promises to claim...

Any sin to confess and forsake...

Any new thought about God...

Any principle to apply to our life, family, job, church, community, or nation...

What specific changes do I need to make...

How exactly will I make them...

What scripture can I memorize to summarize this truth...

What illustration will help me remember it...

Speaking:

Pray for God's manifest Presence.

Pray that the Lord Jesus will be Promoted.

Pray for supernatural Power to do the will of God.

Pray for daily Provisions.

Pray for Protection.

Pray for People.

Pray God will crush our Pride.

Pray for Purity.

Review Positional truth – We are Deeply loved no matter what; Completely forgiven; Fully pleasing; Totally accepted in Christ; Entirely a new creature; Adequately empowered by God's Spirit; etc.

Considering **words**

We need to consider the Dictionary meaning of a Word. This can be discovered by looking at various translations; or by getting a Bible dictionary; and getting into original languages.

Discovering the grammatical tenses, etc. This is not always possible without the right kind of tools and training but don't worry about it! It's like watching a movie in black and white versus watching a movie in color. It might be more pleasing to watch it in color, but you get the same movie even if it's in black and white.

An important thing to watch for is *pronoun changes.*

For example take Heb. 6:1-8:

¹ Therefore leaving the principles of the doctrine of Christ, let us go on unto perfection; not laying again the foundation of repentance from dead works, and of faith toward God, ² Of the doctrine of baptisms, and of laying on of hands, and of resurrection of the dead, and of eternal judgment. ³ And this will we do, if God permit. ⁴ For *it is* impossible for those who were once enlightened, and have tasted of the heavenly gift, and were made partakers of the Holy Ghost, ⁵ And have tasted the good word of God, and the powers of the world to come, ⁶ If they shall fall away, to renew them again unto repentance; seeing they crucify to themselves the Son of God afresh, and put *him* to an open shame. ⁷ For the earth which drinks in the rain that cometh oft upon it, and brings forth herbs meet for them by whom it is dressed, receives blessing from God: ⁸ But that which bears thorns and briers *is* rejected, and *is* nigh unto

cursing; whose end *is* to be burned. Hebrews 6:1-8

The *Case* given [Five participles in the Greek text]

It is impossible for those who were once enlightened, this takes place at conversion (Heb. 10:32).

And it says they have tasted the heavenly gift, referring to experiencing the indwelling Christ (2:9, the *"taste"* means to experience).

It declares that they have become partakers of the Holy Spirit- a reference to the ministry of the Holy Spirit (3:1, 14; 12:8).

And that they have tasted the good word of God and the powers of the age to come – experienced the gospel which was confirmed to them by apostolic miracles (2:4, 9).

Now it speaks of, if they fall away. This is also a participle, grammatically it can be conditional, but it does not have to be. Since all the other participles are unconditional, it is only consistent to make this one unconditional.

The Case given appears to be that of a genuine believer who apostatizes by turning away from Christ.

Homer Kent, "Because of the stated impossibility of renewal, it seems most certain that the reference is to apostasy, that is, a complete and final repudiation of Christ [as in 10:26-27). Hence the normal understanding of these descriptive terms, in the light of the author's own usage elsewhere in the epistle, is of those who are regenerated and then repudiated Christ and forsake Him."

The *Consequences* - For it is impossible...to renew them again to repentance – if his hearers had actually fallen away there would have been no value in talking to them about it!

The *Cause* - since they crucify again for themselves the Son of God, and put *Him* to an open shame – how could one crucify for themselves the Son of God? "Again we have to understand the cultural setting. Paul is addressing this to Jewish believers, before 70 AD. I believe it speaks of going back to the animal sacrifices, which were a type of Christ. The additional description of "put him to open shame" emphasizes the shameful character of apostasy. By renouncing Christ, they would bring more public shame upon Him than if they had never believed at all. Now we see the reason for the impossibility of repentance. They have already tried everything God has to offer, and have then turned away from it. Hence there is nothing further that can be done for them. There will be no additional gospel, no new Messiah. To turn away from God's plan of salvation is to reject the only valid plan there is." These are *true* believers who were *contemplating* going back to the animal sacrifice that is Judaism to avoid persecution.

"They being genuine believers could *not* actually turn away from Jesus Christ's Person and Word by going back to the animal sacrifices. But they could think about it, though they obviously did not think through the implications of such a return. All they were focusing on was the severe persecution at the hands of the Jews, a persecution that would cease if they went back to Judaism. The author of Hebrews is confronting them with the seriousness and foolishness of their thinking. If they went back to the animal sacrifices they would be saying that Jesus' sacrifice was not sufficient. It would be going from the substance to the shadow. He is forcing them to take their thoughts to their logical conclusion, something which they had not done. Since the sacrifices depicted Christ's final sacrifice, it would be like constantly crucifying Christ. Again, this apostasy would *not* be possible for a genuine believer, but they needed to be confronted with their foolishness and move onto maturity."

Pronoun Change

Proof for this is:

The Pronoun change. Notice *before* the warning the pronouns, 5:11-6:3, "we...you... you...you...etc. Then the warning itself, 6:4-8, "those…them…they." And then after the warning it's back to "we…you…etc." This proves this is but a hypothetical warning to them.

After the warning passage he says, "We are convinced of better things concerning you, things that accompany salvation, though we speak in this way. V.9

Verse 10 shows that they were identified with the ground that bore fruit not the thorns of verse 7.

7 For the earth which drinketh in the rain that cometh oft upon it, and bringeth forth herbs meet for them by whom it is dressed, receiveth blessing from God: 8 But that which beareth thorns and briers *is* rejected, and *is* nigh unto cursing; whose end *is* to be burned. Hebrews 6:7-8

VV. 11-20 give them great assurance of their security.

Hypothetical cases are found in scripture. See, Jn. 9:39/ Gal. 3:12/ Ja. 2:10 / etc.

Ryrie, "Others understand the passage to be a warning to genuine believers to urge them on in the Christian growth and maturity. To "fall away" is impossible [since, according to this view, true believers are eternally secure], but the phrase is placed in the sentence to strengthen the warning. It is similar to saying something like this to a class of students: "It is impossible for a student, once enrolled in this course, if he turns the clock back [which cannot be done] to start the course over. Therefore, let all students go on to deeper knowledge."

Point, considering the pronoun change is key is to understanding that passage. It often is…

The Commentaries

If you can get some commentaries, they can be helpful, unless they become a crutch to where you cannot study without them.

So all this is under Interpretation – Context, Cross-reference; Culture; and Considering words.

Questions

Bombard the text with questions: Who? What? Where? When? Why? How? So What? Write down the questions and seek to answer them, but at this stage asking is more important than answering them. Who are these people in my passage? What is the basic purpose of the passage? Where did all of this take place? When did they take place? Etc. I have watched a kid's show many times with my grandkids called Curious George; it's about a monkey whose curiosity is always getting him into trouble. Our trouble is a lack of curiosity!

Integration

The theological framework puts the passage in light of the overall teaching of the Bible. Systematic theology is an organized study of all the passages that relate to a Biblical subject.

Imagination - write the passage out in your own words.

Injection – we need to inject the gospel into every sermon.

Incubation – sleep on it! Give the Holy Spirit time to do His work. Brood over the Scriptures and He will birth some wonderful ideas.

Application

General:

Examples to follow?

Exhortations to obey?

Promises to claim?

Sin to confess or forsake?

Error to avoid?

Any new principles to apply?

Any new thoughts about God?

Specific:

How does this apply to my life; family; work; church; community; and Nation?

What specific changes do I need to make?

How exactly will I go about making this change?

What verse could I memorize that would best summarize this truth?

What illustration can I use to help me remember this truth?

What hymn would help me remember this truth?

I have bought many Muscle and Fitness magazines through the years, though not in recent years. I used to love to read those articles on how to lift weights, as long as I was lifting my weights! From time to time I quit lifting and guess what, during those times I lose interest in those magazines, I never even open them. But the moment I start lifting weights, I start reading them again. Why? Because I knew I was going to apply what I read. It is the same with the Bible! If you are not applying the Word of God to your life, you will lose all interest in God's Word. It is obedience to God's Word that compels us into God's Word and really causes us to be educated in the things of God.

Implementation

We must have a determination to obey. Sometimes we pastors are the most guilty of not applying the Word of God. It reminds me of a doctor, a lawyer, and a preacher who went hunting together. A deer jumped out in front of them and all shot at it. The deer immediately went down. When they came to it there was no bullet hole! They begin to argue about which one shot the deer. About that time a game warden came by and asked what the problem was. They explained it to him and he examined the deer. He said, "It was the preacher who killed the deer." The doctor asked, "How do you know?" He said, "Because the bullet went in one ear, and out the other!" We must not allow God's Word to simply go in one ear and out the other.

Illustration - Find an illustration that will help you to remember this truth.

Invocation - Find a hymn that will help you worship this truth.

Interaction - Share your study with someone.

Ok, let us look at something practical, an Introduction and the conclusion.

The *Startling* introduction

Get their attention. Use an illustration; quote; Joke; Startling statement; Personal experience; background of a hymn; Scripture; etc.

Meet a basic need, a longing; craving; want; desire; ambition; hunger; etc.

Give your one simple statement that has the subject and the compliment.

The *Stopping* of the sermon

Review the main points.

Restate the dominate theme.

Land the plane! Use an illustration; quote; personal experience; etc.

I appreciate the opportunity to be here this week, and I want to encourage you to make Bible study a priority in your life. You may not have access to many commentaries and other books. Just remember the words of John Bunyan who wrote *Pilgrim's Progress*:

"Although you may have no commentaries at hand, continue to read the Word and pray; for a little from God is better than a great deal received from a man. Too many are content to listen to what comes from men's mouths, without searching and kneeling before God to know the real truth. That which we receive directly from the Lord through the study of His Word is from the 'minting house' itself. Even old truths are new if they come to us with the smell of heaven upon them."

I would recommend that you make a copy of the quick overview. Run it off on colored paper using extra thick paper. That makes it easy to find and will last much longer then just normal paper.

Quick Overview:

Inspiration – that the Bible is God breathed.

Illumination – the revealing ministry of the Holy Spirit.

Intercession – from beginning to end it must be bathed in prayer.

Investigation – (Observation) Reading and Reflecting.

Identification – of a Theme and Outline.

Interpretation – Context; Cross-references; Cultural setting; Considering words; Consultation; Commentaries.

Interrogation – bombard the text with questions.

Integration – what is the theological framework.

Imagination – write out the passage in your own words.

Injection – of the gospel.

Incubation – to brood over the scriptures until the Holy Spirit births a communication to your spirit. Involves contemplation, prayer, meditation.

Implication – (Application) how does this apply to my life?

Implementation – a determination to obey.

Illustration - to help remember this truth.

Invocation – find a hymn that relates to your passage.

Interaction – share your study with someone.

Chapter Six

SAMPLING **FROM A STUDY**

What I am attempting to do is present a pattern – these principles applied to Psa. 23, can be applied to any book of the Bible. For a more detailed study on Psa. 23, get my book GPS-23.

FIRST, *INTERPRETATION,* AS WE APPROACH THE PSALM, WE IDENTIFY THE DISPENSATION. It is during the Age of the Law, see previous notes.

ILLUMINATION – Open my eyes that I may behold wondrous things out of your word. Psa. 119:18

INTERCESSION - Pray before, during, and after studying this Psalm.

INVESTIGATION - Read! Read! Read! Use as many translations as you can.

IDENTIFICATION - We seek to identify the dominate thought and outline.

Dominate thought - This is not complicated! We simply read Psa. 23, over and over again, [in as many translations as you can]. As we read it we can see something that the concept of the Lord as the believer's Shepherd is the focus. We might be able to call it *The Shepherd: Sufficient for Life's Journey.*

Now outline the passage: Here is my outline, just to give you an idea, your outline will, of course, be different.

The Shepherd is Phenomenal.

The Shepherd is Perpetual.

The Shepherd is Personal.

The Shepherd gives us the Principle of satisfaction.

The Shepherd is Provisional.

The Shepherd is Peaceful.

The Shepherd reaches out to the Prodigal.

The Shepherd makes righteousness Possible.

The Shepherd is there when life turns Painful.

The Shepherd is Practical.

The Shepherd is Plentiful.

The Shepherd's purpose is Pleasurable.

The Shepherd is Promotional.

Intro:

1. Illustration: Always begin a sermon by seeking to set the tone, to get people's interest perked up.

Roy Angell was parked in front of a big city hospital in Miami, he recognized a physician who was coming down the steps and headed for his car. Roy noticed that he was moving his lips as if talking. As he walked by my car I said, "Bascom, you are too young to be talking to yourself." He smiled and said, "I wasn't talking to myself. I was saying the twenty-third Psalm. I just came from the room of a little old saint on the fourth floor who can't live much longer. She asked me if I knew the twenty-third Psalm. When I told her I claimed it as my very own and that I leaned on it every day, she replied, 'Let's say it together. This twenty-third Psalm has been enshrined on a marble pedestal too long. We need to take it down and break it up and use it. It's something to live with and live by."

2. How true! Someone rightly said familiarity breeds contempt; we are so familiar with this Psalm that we have allowed it to slip into useless obscurity.

3. The Shepherd is Sufficient for Life's Journey.

Trans: Psa. 23

Note that things like the belief in Inspiration; trusting the Holy Spirit for Illumination; Intercession; Incubation; an attitude to make Implementation; and Interaction of this truth with others is something that the student should be making on his own. Also note that this is not meant to be an exhaustive study, only a sample, and many questions will not be addressed because of the limited scope of this study.

I. FIRST, THE SHEPHERD IS *PHENOMENAL*.

Phenomenal means, "highly extraordinary; remarkable; amazingly unprecedented."

Investigation: This is done by reading, and reading, and reading. Take that first verse, "The Lord is my shepherd, I shall not want." It is often helpful to read it in various translations:

"THE LORD is my Shepherd [to feed, guide, and shield me], I shall not lack." Psalm 23:1 (AMP)

" Because the Lord is my Shepherd, I have everything I need!" Psalm 23:1 (TLB)

"The Lord takes care of me as his sheep; I will not be without any good thing." Psalm 23:1 (BBE)

As you read it over and over again you start to get a feel for the passage. Our investigation causes us to read carefully each word and reflect upon it.

The LORD [3068s] – Yahweh, this is a *proper name* for God. The numbers are related to Strong's Concordance. Strong's Concordance: If you look up the word "Lord" which is listed in alphabetical order. You will find the word "LORD" and off to the far right you will see the number *3068*. Go to the back of this concordance and under *HEBREW AND ARAMAIC DICTIONARY* and simply look up the number 3068.

Interpretation: Context of this Psalm.

Psa. 22, speaks of the Death of the Messiah, the Lord Jesus Christ. Reminding us of the Good Shepherd who died for His sheep (Jn. 10:11)

Psa. 23, speaks of the Messiah taking care of His people. Reminding us of the Great Shepherd who lives for His sheep. (Heb. 13:20-21)

Psa. 24, speaks of Messiah's coming for His People. Reminding us of the Chief Shepherd who will return for His sheep (1 Pet. 5:4).

Interpretation: Cross-Reference.

The personal name of the living God found 6,823 times in the Old Testament. It would be impossible to look up such a vast number of verses.

"In the Hebrew language the word translated 'I am' is related to the name Yahweh. Originally, Hebrew was written with consonants only, and the readers put in the vowels as they read. Most believed that 'Yahweh' is the correct pronunciation of the word YHWH (the name of Israel's God); though absolute certainty is not possible, as there are no Hebrew records old enough to preserve the original pronunciation. By the time it had become the practice to add the vowels in written Hebrew; the Jews no longer spoke the name YHWH. They claimed this showed their reverence for the holy name of God, but for many it was more a superstition. Whatever the reason, the practice developed that when Jews read the Scriptures, instead of speaking the word YHWH, they substituted the word *adonai*, meaning 'lord' or 'master'. When the Hebrew Bible added vowels to the consonants for the first time (about 300 BC), it put the vowels of *adonai* to the consonants YHWH. This was pronounced Jehovah; translators of English versions of the Bible usually avoid the pronunciation problem by using the expression 'the LORD' (in capital letters) as the substitute for YHWH."

One of the most important passages related to this Name is found in Ex. 3:14. Unger's New Bible Dictionary "The passage in Exodus 3:14 seems to furnish designedly a clue to the meaning of the word. When Moses received his commission..."God said to Moses, "I AM WHO I AM." And He said, "Thus you shall say to the children of Israel, I AM has sent me to you." YHWH, the root idea is that of *underived existence.* When it is said that God's name is *He Is,* simply being is not all that is affirmed. *He is* in a sense in which no other being *is.* *He is,* and the cause of His being is in Himself."

Interpretation: Consultation.

Kenneth Boa, "God is exalted so far above the created universe that we cannot even imagine it. He is not only lofty and eminent; He stands apart from His creation in a different quality of being. He is the blessed and only Ruler, the King of kings and Lord of lords, who alone is immortal and who lives in unapproachable light, whom no man has seen or can see."

James Montgomery Boice, "It is an inexhaustible name, like its bearer. Chiefly, it refers to God's timelessness, on the one hand, and to his self-sufficiency, on the other. Self-sufficiency means that God needs nothing. He needs no wisdom from anyone else; he has all wisdom with himself. He needs no power; He is all-powerful. He does not need to be worshipped or helped or served. Nor is He accountable to anyone. He answers only to Himself. Timelessness means that God is always the same in these eternal traits or attributes. He was like this yesterday; He will be like this tomorrow. He will be unchanged and unchangeable forever. He is the great "I AM."

F..B. Meyer, "All other life, from the [bug] on the rose-leaf to the archangel before the throne, is dependent and derived. All others waste, and change, and grow old; He only is unchangeable the same…He alone is self-sustained. That mighty Being is our Shepherd."

Lucado, "Yahweh – an unchanging God…Relationships change. Health changes. The weather changes. But the Yahweh who ruled the earth last night is the same Yahweh who rules it today. Same plan. Same mood. Same love. He never changes …No one breathed life into Yahweh. No one gave birth to Him. No one caused Him. No act brought Him forth. Though He creates, God was never created. Though He causes, He was never caused… Since no act brought Him forth, no act can take Him out…Yahweh is not troubled by anything – cancer does not trouble

Him and cemeteries do not disturb Him…You don't need to carry the burden of a lesser god…a god on a shelf, a god in a box, a god in a bottle. No, you need a God who can place 100 billion stars in our galaxy and 100 billion galaxies in the universe. You need a God who can shape two fists of flesh into 75 or 100 billion nerve cells, each with as many as 10,000 connections to other nerve cells, place it in a skull, and call it a brain….You need Yahweh!"

Interrogation:

Who is Yahweh? My Shepherd!

What does He mean to me? That will become clear as we work our way through this Psalm.

Where can He be found? Anywhere, anyplace, anytime;

When do I need Him? When don't I need Him!

Why is He vital to me? He is the source of my existence and continuance.

How can I know Him? Look up Jn. 17:3/ 1 Jn. 5:11-13/.

So What? It means I have a reference point in life. I know Where I came from; Who I am; Why I am here; and Where I am going.

Integration:

Charles Ryrie has a good overview:

Origin of the Word

The name apparently comes from the root *hawa*, which signifies either existence (as of a tree trunk where it falls, Eccles. 11:3) or development (as in Neh. 6:6). Perhaps both ideas can be combined in the significance of God's name by saying that it denotes Him as the active, self-existent One.

Revelation of the Name

This name was used by Eve (Gen. 4:1), people in the days of Seth (v. 26), Noah (9:26), and Abraham (12:8; 15:2, 8). But it was to Moses that the deep significance of the name was revealed. God said that even though He appeared to the patriarchs

He was not known to them by His name *Yahweh* (Exod. 6:3). The meaning of the name was not known in its fullest and deepest sense. This revelation came to Moses at the burning bush when God identified Himself as "I AM WHO I AM" (3:14), the principal idea being that God was present with the people of Israel.

Sacredness of the Name

Since *Yahweh* was God's personal name by which He was known to Israel, in post-exilic times it began to be considered so sacred that it was not pronounced. Instead the term *Adonai* was usually substituted, and by the sixth to seventh centuries A.D. the vowels of *Adonai* were combined with the consonants *YHWH* to remind the synagogue reader to pronounce the sacred name as *Adonai*. From this came the artificial word *Jehovah.* But all of this underscores the awe in which the name was held.

Significance of the Name

Several facets seem to be included in the significance of the name *Yahweh*.

1. It emphasizes God's changeless self-existence. This may be supported by the etymology and from the Lord's use of Exodus 3:14 in John 8:58 to state His claim to absolute eternal existence.

2. It assures God's presence with His people. See Exodus 3:12.

3. It is connected with God's power to work on behalf of His people and to keep His covenant with them, which was illustrated and confirmed by His work in their deliverance from Egypt (Exod. 6:6).

Compounds with the Name

1. Yahweh Jireh, "the Lord Will Provide" (Gen. 22:14). After the Angel of the Lord pointed to a ram to use as a substitute for Isaac, Abraham named the place "the Lord Will Provide."

2. Yahweh Nissi, "the Lord is My Banner" (Exod. 17:15). After the defeat of the Amalekites, Moses erected an altar and called it *Yahweh Nissi*.

3. Yahweh Shalom, "the Lord is Peace" (Judg. 6:24).

4. Yahweh Sabbaoth, "the Lord of hosts" (1 Sam. 1:3). This is a military figure that pictures *Yahweh* as the Commander of the angelic armies of heaven as well as the armies of Israel (1 Sam. 17:45). The title reveals the sovereignty and omnipotence of God and was used often by the prophets (Isaiah and Jeremiah) to remind the people during times of national crisis that God was their Leader and Protector.

5. Yahweh Maccaddeshcem, "the Lord who sanctifies you" (Exod. 31:13).

6. Yahweh Roi, "the Lord is my shepherd" (Ps. 23:1).

7. Yahweh Tsidkenu, "the Lord our righteousness" (Jer. 23:6).

8. Yahweh Shammah, "the Lord is there" (Ezek. 48:35).

9. *Yahweh Elohim Israel* "the Lord, the God of Israel" (Judg. 5:3; Isa. 17:6).

Strictly speaking, these compounds are not additional names of God, but designations or titles that often grew out of commemorative events. However, they do reveal additional facets of the character of God.
[Basic Theology: A Popular Systematic Guide to Understanding Biblical Truth]

Implication:

He never changes! He is the only reliable reference point in life. Everything and everybody else is in flux, they change and go downhill. Not Him!

Illustration:

When Lloyd Douglas author of *The Robe* went to school, he lived in a boardinghouse. He recalls a music professor who was confined to a wheel chair living in the same place. He asked him "What's good news?" The professor grabbed his tuning fork and tapped the side of his wheel chair. "That is middle C. It was middle C yesterday; it will be middle C tomorrow; it will be middle C a thousand years from now! The tenor upstairs sings flat. The piano across the hall is out of tune, but, my friend, that is middle C." In this changing and unstable world we desperately need a middle C, something that can be depended upon, that remains the same – that is Yahweh!

Invocation: Music to jog the Memory!

I stand amazed in the presence of Jesus the Nazarene,

and wonder how He could love me,

a sinner, condemned, unclean.

Refrain:

How marvelous! How wonderful!

And my song shall ever be:

How marvelous! How wonderful

is my Savior's love for me!

Well, you get the idea; I love this twenty-third psalm so much I wrote a book about it, GPS-23. Anyway, just keep on working through it until you have come to the end. Yes, it is a lot of work, but it is well worth the effort.

Chapter Seven

***STAYING* WITH STUDYING**

William Carey was born in 1761, as a child he had persistent problems with *allergies.* He was a *shoemaker* from the age of 16 to 28. At the age of 20 he *married*, it was a disaster as she was totally disinterested in her husband's passion for the souls of *India.* He accepted a call to become the *pastor* of a small Baptist church, but was determined to go to the mission field.
His *father* called him "mad" and his *wife* violently opposed leaving her homeland. He was told that he had no academic qualifications that would fit him for the work. However, he said, "*I can plod."* He finally left for India with a fellow missionary and his 8-year-old son, but the ship was forced to turn back for technical reasons.

Later, his wife reluctantly agreed to go with him. Once in India the family faced one hardship after another, living in utter poverty. His wife lost her health - both mentally and physically. In fact, one co-worker labeled her "mentally deranged." His son died, and at the end of *7 years* he did not even have one convert. But he worked diligently to translate the Bible into the people's language. In *1812*, a priceless manuscript was destroyed in a fire, along with a huge multilingual dictionary, and some needed grammar books. Yet he persisted onward. William Carey once said, "I can plod. I can persevere in any definite pursuit. To this I owe everything."

Webster's Dictionary defines plodding as, "to proceed slowly or tediously, to work laboriously and forwardly."

The Staying Studying.

Therefore, my beloved brethren, be ye stedfast, unmoveable, always abounding in the work of the Lord, forasmuch as ye know that your labour is not in vain in the Lord. 1 Corinthians 15:58

We see the *Mystery*

Therefore - the conjunction takes us back to the context.

First, that takes us to the *Rapture*. 1 Cor. 15:51-56

[51] Behold, I show you a mystery; We shall not all sleep, but we shall all be changed, [52] In a moment, in the twinkling of an eye, at the last trump: for the trumpet shall sound, and the dead shall be raised incorruptible, and we shall be changed. [53] For this corruptible must put on incorruption, and this mortal *must* put on immortality. [54] So when this corruptible shall have put on incorruption, and this mortal shall have put on immortality, then shall be brought to pass the saying that is written, Death is swallowed up in victory. [55] O death, where *is* thy sting? O grave, where *is* thy victory? [56] The sting of death *is* sin; and the strength of sin *is* the law. 1 Corinthians 15:51-56

Many people don't talk much about the rapture these days; I suppose it's because of all these nuts setting dates for it. I'm like G. Campbell Morgan who, after giving a sermon on the rapture, was approached by a man who said:

"I just can't get that out of the scriptures." He said, "Of course you can't - it's there to stay!" I believe one thing that keeps us plodding for God is the "blessed hope" that any moment we may be snatched out of here!

[16] For the Lord himself shall descend from heaven with a shout, with the voice of the archangel, and with the trump of God: and the dead in Christ shall rise first: [17] Then we which are alive *and* remain shall be caught up together with them in the clouds, to meet the Lord in the air: and so shall we ever be with the Lord. [18]Wherefore comfort one another with these words. 1 Thessalonians 4:16-18 See Rev. 3:10

Dwight L. Moody used to say, "I never preach a sermon without thinking that possibly the Lord may come before I preach another."

G. Campbell Morgan said, "I never begin my work in the morning without thinking that perhaps God may interrupt my work and begin His own. I am not looking for death. I am looking for Him."

Martin Luther said he only had two days on his calendar—today and "that day."

Alexander McLaren, "The ancient church thought a great deal more about the coming of Jesus Christ than about death - to them the way of passing out of life was not so much seeing corruption as being caught up together in the air."

Billy Sunday, "The Christian has no business looking for death...instead of expecting to go to the grave, he should be looking for a meeting in the air."

Bonar, as he drew the curtains closed at night repeated to himself the words, "Perhaps tonight, Lord!" In the morning, as he awoke and greeted a new day said, "Perhaps today, Lord!" He expected the Lord to return, every day, of his 60 years of ministry.

[8] Henceforth there is laid up for me a crown of righteousness, which the Lord, the righteous judge, shall give me at that day: and not to me only, but unto all them also that love his appearing. 2 Timothy 4:8

When *Harry Truman* became President, he was concerned about losing touch with the common everyday American. So he would often go out and be among them. Once he took a walk down to the *Memorial Bridge* on the *Potomac River*. He came upon a man who was eating his lunch. The man looked up, not in the least surprised, smiled and said, "You know, Mr. President, I was just thinking about you!"

I hope the rapture won't take us by surprise, I hope we will be able to say, "Lord, I was just thinking about You!"

Next, the *Victor*

But thanks *be* to God, which gives us the victory through our Lord Jesus Christ. 1 Corinthians 15:57

The Victor is God, "Thanks be *to God who gives us the victory*" who gives victory "*through our Lord Jesus Christ.*"

Since we have the victor, we have victory and that enables us to plod for God. Victory is a Person!

But thanks be to God, Who gives us the victory [making us conquerors] through our Lord Jesus Christ." 1 Corinthians 15:57 (AMP)

Yet in all these things we are more than conquerors through Him who loved us." Romans 8:37

We are not conquerors - we are *more than* conquerors. Michael Spinks was a heavyweight boxing champion at one time. He prepared hard to fight Larry Holmes - jumping rope; running; speed bag; punching bag; sparring for hours on end. In 1985, he fought a grueling 15 round fight with Larry Holmes and won by a unanimous decision. He was a conqueror! I do not know how much he was paid for that fight - let's say 1 million dollars. Now Michael Spink's wife, Sandy, sticks out her bony hand and he hands her 1 million dollars. She is *more* than a conqueror.

Interestingly Spinks said after the fight, "Thank God. I asked Him to take over. All I did was let Him use my body. You know, I never saw myself winning this." See, Rom. 8:13

Of course, this doesn't eliminate our need to say "No" to sin, God never eliminates our responsibility to say no. But just saying no is like trying to hold up a watch - will power will not beat sin power.

But we say "no" and then trust the Holy Spirit to make that no stick through the sufficiency of Jesus Christ.

The *Mandatory*

We have to know that we are *Beloved.*

my beloved – whatever we face in life we must be assured that God loves us no matter what. And He does! Rom.

5:8 is proof of His unconditional and unending love. Imagine holding up a 100 dollar bill. I ask, "Who would like this $100 bill?" Obviously hands go up everywhere! Now suppose I take it and crumple it up and then ask, "Who wants it now?" You can bet the same hands will be raised. Then I drop it to the floor and step on it and it gets all dirty. Now I ask, "Who still wants it?" The same hands go up in the air. Why? Because it is still worth 100 dollars! God loves us not because of something we have done, but because He put us into union with Christ. He has made you a new creature and loves you no matter what.

We also have to be a *Believer.*

Brother – God's love is blocked by our sin until we place our trust in Jesus Christ and receive Him as our Savior (Jn. 1:12).

According to writers Kent McDill and Melissa Isaacson, Don Calhoun worked for five dollars an hour at an office supply store in Bloomington, Illinois. He had attended two Chicago Bulls basketball games in his life, and now he was going to his third. When he strolled into Chicago Stadium, a woman who worked for the Bulls organization walked up to him and told him they were selecting him to take part in a promotional event during the game called the Million Dollar Shot. The Shot came after a time-out in the third quarter. If Calhoun could shoot a basket standing seventy-nine feet away—that means he had to stand behind the free throw line on the opposite end of the court and throw the ball three quarters of the length of the court—he would win one million dollars. Calhoun played basketball at the Bloomington YMCA, but he had never tried a shot like this before. He took the basketball in his hands and looked over at Michael Jordan and the rest of the Bulls. He could see they were pulling for him. Calhoun stepped to the line and let fly. As soon as the basketball left his hand, coach Phil Jackson said, "It's good." Indeed, the ball went through the basket in a swish. The stadium crowd went wild. Calhoun rushed into the arms of

Michael Jordan, and the Bulls players crowded around slapping him on the back. When Don Calhoun went home that night, he had only two dollars in his wallet, but he would receive fifty thousand dollars a year for the next twenty years of his life. Sometimes one action, one decision, one moment can change everything for you. So it is when you choose to receive Christ into your life.

The *Mentality*

be steadfast, unmovable

First, we have to deal with - *Temptations.*

steadfast - it speaks of that which is stationary. We stand firm against sin, sin nature, Satan...How? Remember 1 Cor. 15:57

TDNT, "That which is steadfast is what endures in every change and contradiction. But where in the whole world is there anything that can be called steadfast, that has the guarantee of permanence by nature? There is only one who stands fast, namely He who is in heaven. There is only one thing which persists in the flux of occurrence, namely His creative and overruling hand. If anything stands fast on earth, it must be established by God, owing its steadfastness, its permanence, its ability to withstand assault solely to Him."

Let's be clear - we are not talking about being steadfast only when we prevail, but when we fail! Truthfully is we all know what it's like to fail. The Bible is filled with failure! If you eliminate the murderers from the Bible you would lose a good bit of it! Moses, David, and Paul all committed murder! Peter denied the Lord, but he didn't quit, he was the key-note speaker on the Day of Pentecost. We are not like Judas who failed and then went out and hanged himself! There are plenty of people who will give you the rope.

[8] If we say that we have no sin, we deceive ourselves, and the truth is not in us. [9] If we confess our sins, he is faithful and just to forgive us *our* sins,

and to cleanse us from all unrighteousness. 1 John 1:8-9

Admit it; quit it; and forget it!

I remember Bill Stafford once said, "Every now and then the devil sneaks up on my blind side and knocks me down. But I look at him and say, "I'll be up in the morning!" We must remain steadfast even after we fall short of the glory of God! We continue to plod for God!

Furthermore, we have to deal with - *Tribulations*.

unmovable - means "to stir up; shake; disturb; agitate." With an alpha prefix, which negates it. We refuse to be shaken by people, circumstances, whatever. Life is filled with problems and "all that live godly in Christ Jesus will suffer persecution." You may be as righteous as Job, but you will suffer at times like Job - health problems; family problems; church problems; financial problems...Storms are part of life!

²² And now, behold, I go bound in the spirit unto Jerusalem, not knowing the things that shall befall me there: ²³ Save that the Holy Ghost witnesseth in every city, saying that bonds and afflictions abide me. ²⁴ But none of these things move me, neither count I my life dear unto myself, so that I might finish my course with joy, and the ministry, which I have received of the Lord Jesus, to testify the gospel of the grace of God. Acts 20:22-24 (KJV)

Paul knew how to plod for God...

A few years ago, on one of the Monday Night Football telecasts, the sportscasters were discussing the great running backs of professional football history, one of whom was Walter Payton of the Chicago Bears. He was the all-time leading ground gainer in the National Football League. Frank Gifford said, "What a runner! Do you realize that all together, Walter Payton gained more than 9 miles rushing in his career? Just imagine that—more than 9 miles!" To which the other sportscaster, Dan Dierdorff, responded: "And to think that every

4.6 yards of the way, someone was knocking him down." There will always be something or someone who knocks you down, yet the key is to keep getting back up! Keep plodding for God...

The *Ministry*

always abounding in the work of the Lord - several things here.

First, a ministry *Exists.*

Today in America we have a high unemployment rate but the unemployment rate for the church is always 0%! Every believer has a *spiritual gift*! Every one of us has been given a work to do.

For we are his workmanship, created in Christ Jesus unto good works, which God hath before ordained that we should walk in them. Ephesians 2:10

According to 1 Cor. 12:4-6, God determines the What, Where, and How related to spiritual gifts.

You, as a preacher of God's Word, have been afforded the greatest privilege that can be given to a human being:

Wilbur Smith, "God has a plan for every life, and men can serve the Lord just as heartily and helpfully in the marketplace and banking house as in the pulpit, but blessed is the man who feels in his heart the urge to preach the gospel. Your speaker makes this confession. He would rather be the pastor of the smallest Baptist church you know, even if considered a failure by his friends, than to occupy some high position and be considered a success."

Alexander Whyte, "The angels around the throne envy you and your great work."

Dr. Martyn Lloyd-Jones who left a promising medical career to enter teaching God's Word said, "I gave up nothing; I received everything. I count it the highest honor that God can confer on any man to call him to be a herald of [God's Word]."

Ray Stedman, "I became aware of a growing sense in my own life of the grandeur of preaching. Of what I have called the majesty of ministry...I have felt a deeply humbling conviction that I will never be given a greater honor than what has already been given to me, that I should preach the unsearchable riches of Christ."

Furthermore, we are to *Excel.*

always abounding - the word means "to excel, to go above and beyond."

"...Always give yourselves fully to the work of the Lord" (NIV)

"...Always keep busy working for the Lord." 1 Corinthians 15:58 (CEV)

"...And don't hold back. Throw yourselves into the work of the Master" 1 Corinthians 15:58 (MSG)

The idea is not speaking of *results* but firm *resolve* to give ourselves fully to what God has called us to do. Too easy to focus on *Effects* instead of our *Efforts* - had Noah focused on Effects, he would have stopped building that Ark! He gave it his all for 120 years, without any response at all...

When Billy Graham went to Africa he drew crowds of 10,000 people. And yet David Livingstone ministered there for years and saw very little response.

Livingstone, "Future missionaries will see conversions following every sermon. We prepared the way for them. May they not forget the pioneers who worked in the *thick gloom* with few rays to cheer except as flow from faith in God's promise. We worked for a glorious future which we are not destined to see."

Read Heb. 11:35b-40 and you will find people who were abounding in the work of the Lord with very little results...

Billy Graham back in 1960 met with 25 missionaries during his African crusades. He shared with them how thousands had gathered to hear him proclaim the gospel. He then asked them about their ministry. Billy writes:

"I sensed that most of them were somewhat embarrassed, for we had just been talking about the large crowds and the unexpected response we had seen almost everywhere. But one by one they quietly told of their work. Some of them had been laboring for years, with almost nothing in the way of tangible results. And yet, they each had a deep sense that this was where God had called them; and that was all they needed to know. Tears welled up in our eyes as we prayed with them in the attitude of 1 Cor. 3:, "Neither he who plants nor he who waters is anything but God who causes the increase."

You have a ministry; it is God-given and is just as important as any other ministry regardless of the size! Excel in it! Give your all and leave the results in God's hand.

We should have the attitude about our ministry as inventor Thomas Edison. His wife repeatedly urged him to take a vacation from his demanding work to which he gave himself unreservedly. Finally, he agreed. He asked his wife, "Where should I go?" She replied, "Where you would rather be, more than anywhere else on earth? Go there." He agreed, "All right, I will go tomorrow." The next morning he got up and went back to work in his laboratory.

We are to *Magnify* God

Your labor is not in vain in the Lord - it is not empty, it is not for naught. It is for the glory of God and it will be rewarded (Heb.11:6).

[31] Whether therefore you eat, or drink, or whatsoever ye do, do all to the glory of God. 1 Corinthians 10:31

[10] As every man hath received the gift, *even so* minister the same one to another, as good stewards of the manifold grace of God. [11] If any man speak, *let him speak* as the oracles of God; if any man minister, *let him do it* as of the ability which God gives: that God in all things may be glorified through Jesus Christ, to whom be praise and dominion for ever and ever. Amen. 1 Peter 4:10-11

Any other motive will prove to be vain, empty - glorifying and promoting self is the curse of the day!

I *am* the LORD: that *is* my name: and my glory will I not give to another, neither my praise to graven images. Isaiah 42:8

I read about a *ministering band* that traveled from town to town in Europe. Attendance had been low and they were discouraged. That night it was snowing, and they were not expecting many to attend. One member said, "Why don't we just cancel tonight." Most in the band agreed, but one of them said. "No, we have a responsibility to minister to those few who might venture out. I think we should give them our best." Reluctantly they all agreed and as expected the turnout was pitiful, but they played their hearts out. A few days later they received a letter, "Thank you for a beautiful performance." Signed, Your King.

We minister for the King of kings and the Lord of lords and that should be motivation enough!

One went to hear one preacher after another, leaving saying, "What a preacher!" Then he heard Spurgeon and left saying, "What a Savior!" The focus is not on us - it's on Jesus!

Ruth Graham wrote, "Pashi, from India was a college student. When he was presented with the claims of Christ, Pashi told me, "I would like to believe in Christ. But we have never seen a Christian who was like Christ." I asked Dr. Haqq, a brilliant Christian who had been president of a school of Islamic studies in India, "How would you answer Pashi? What would you say?" He said, "That is simple, I would tell Pashi, I am not offering you Christians. I am offering you Christ."

Two things: First, only Jesus Christ ever lived a perfect life; and second, nobody was saved by His life, that could only expose our imperfection and sin. People are saved by trusting in His substitutionary death and resurrection; If nobody was ever saved by his perfect life, what makes us think our imperfect life is going to save anyone? We do seek to live a godly Christian life, but that is not our gospel or our focus!!! We will not glorify ourselves and plod for God...

Bottom line is this - we are called on to Plod for God.

Paderewski was asked by a fellow *pianist* if he could be ready to play a recital on short notice. He replied, "I am always ready. I have practiced 8 hours daily for 40 years." To which the man replied, "I wish I had been born with such determination." Paderewski said, "We were all born with it, I just use mine."

Every single person who has been born-again, has the ability to plod for God, it is a question of appropriating what we already have.

Gospel Presentation:

Let me ask you one of the most important questions you will ever ponder.

Have you come to a place in your life where you know for certain that if you died you would go to heaven?

The only answer to that question is, yes, no, or I don't know. Take a moment and think about it. A follow up question would be:'

If you were standing before God right now and He were to ask, "Why should I let you into my perfect heaven?"

What do you think you would say? You might say, "I go to church. I try to live a good life. I try to keep God's law." Such responses are sincere, and I appreciate your honesty. Most would probably say, "I don't know what I would say." Well, would you like to know? Then read the following carefully.

God Really Does Love You

"For God so loved the world, (put your name here), that He gave His only begotten Son, that whoever believes in Him should not perish but have everlasting life" (John 3:16).

It is natural to question this claim; we tend to wonder how God could love us with all of our problems and hang-ups, yes, you can say it – with all of our sins. My wife and I have had two children. When they were born they did nothing for us! And after they were born, for the first several months they kept us up all hours of the night; we had to change their diapers and feed them. I think most of you know what I'm talking about. However, we did love them. Why? I suppose it was because we had something to do with them being in this world. They are our children; they even looked a little like us – poor kids! You need to realize that God is the one who had everything to do with your coming into this world. Without God you would not even exist! He is the Creator and Sustainer of life. He, in fact, created you in His image and loves you even though you have done nothing to deserve it.

So What's a Fella to Do?

Have you ever felt that your life lacked purpose and meaning? Have these thoughts ever crossed your mind:

Where did I come from?

Why am I here?

Where am I going?

God knows the answer to these questions. He created you with a definite purpose in mind.

"The thief does not come except to steal, and to kill, and to destroy. I have come that they may have life, and that they may have it more abundantly" (John 10:10).

An abundant life is a life of purpose, meaning, and fulfillment. That is what God offers you. This brings up an unavoidable question—what happened! If He loves us and has this great purpose for our life, then why are both concepts so foreign to us? The answer is both profound and very simple.

Sin Separates!

We are all sinners, "for all have sinned and fall short of the glory of God" (Rom. 3:22). We are a sinner by birth. God created Adam and Eve and put them in a garden with only one commandment; they were not to eat of a certain tree. They disobeyed God by taking a bite, and thus they sinned.

Now what kind of babies are two sinful people capable of having? It is the law of biogenesis—like produces like. This is why there is no need to teach children how to tell a lie, but only to teach them positive things like telling the truth. They know how to lie naturally!

The reason for that is that we are all born with a sin nature inherited from Adam.

"Therefore, just as through one man sin entered the world, and death through sin, and thus death spread to all men, because all sinned" (Rom. 5:12).

We are also sinners by behavior. Have you not sinned? The Bible commands us to love God with all our heart, mind, and soul. Have you always done that? Have you ever done that? Have you ever told a lie? Have you ever wanted to? God not only looks at our deeds but at our desires. The Bible clearly declares we have all sinned.

So What?

Here is the answer to the so-what question.

"For the wages of sin is death, but the gift of God is eternal life in Christ Jesus our Lord" (Rom. 6:23).

What we have earned from our sin is death. Death means separation.

There is spiritual death—the separation of the spirit/soul from God. "And the LORD God commanded the man, saying, 'Of every tree of the garden you may freely eat; but of the tree of the knowledge of good and evil you shall not eat, for in the day that you eat of it you shall surely die'" (Gen. 2:16–17). The day they ate of it they did not physically die; that took place many years later. But God said *in the day* you eat of it you will die. They died spiritually that very day.

There is also physical death—the separation of the spirit/soul from the body. "And as it is appointed for men to die once, but after this the judgment" (Heb. 9:27). The fact that everybody dies physically is proof positive that everyone is spiritually dead. If we were not sinners, we would not die. The statistics are rather impressive; one out of every one person dies!

If you die physically while you are spiritually dead, you will die eternally. Eternal death is the eternal separation of the spirit/soul/body from God's goodness, grace, mercy, and blessings. It is to be fully conscious and live in a place the Bible calls the lake of fire. "Then Death and Hades were cast into the lake of fire. This is the second death. And anyone not found written in the Book of Life was cast into the lake of fire" (Rev. 20:14–15).

Question: How can you say one moment that God loves me and then in the next that He condemns me?

Well let us imagine putting on a judge's robe and sitting on the bench. Then the unthinkable happens. Your son, whom you love very much, is brought before you, guilty of a capital offense! The penalty for his crime is death, and the evidence is clear as to his guilt. Would you sentence him to death? If you were a just judge, you would, not because you no longer love him, but in spite of your great love for him. God is holy, righteous, and just, as well as a God of love. This looks like bad news! However, the very word *gospel* means good news, so where is this good news?

Jesus Christ Is God

"In the beginning was the Word, and the Word was with God, and the Word was God" (John 1:1).

This is a great mystery, but the Bible teaches that God became God/man. "And the Word became flesh and dwelt among us, and we beheld His glory, the glory as of the only begotten of the Father, full of grace and truth" (John 1:14).

Jesus Christ the Substitute

The Lord Jesus Christ lived a perfect life and then died in your place. "But God demonstrates His own love toward us, in that while we were still sinners, Christ died for us" (Rom. 5:8 NKJV).

Let us put our judge robe back on for a minute. Imagine after sentencing your boy to be executed, taking off your robe and then voluntarily offering to die in his place. That would make you just and loving at the same time. That is what Jesus Christ actually did for us. We do not understand all of this but must accept it by faith. I do not understand electricity, but I still do not live in the dark. I do not understand how the digestive system works, but I still eat. I do not understand how a brown cow eats green grass and produces white milk. You do not have to understand everything to be saved—just that you are a sinner and that Jesus Christ died for your sin.

He Is Not Here, He Has Risen

"For I delivered to you first of all that which I also received: that Christ died for our sins according to the Scriptures, and that He was buried, and that He rose again the third day according to the Scriptures, and that He was seen by Cephas, then by the twelve. After that He was seen by over five hundred brethren at once, of whom the greater part remain to the present, but some have fallen asleep" (1 Cor. 15:3–6).

By rising from the dead, He proved that He paid for all of our sins. If He had not, death would have held Him. It also proved that He had no sin of His own. If He had, He would have stayed dead like everybody else.

One Way Only

We have all seen *One Way Only* signs, and so it is with the way of salvation. There is only one person who can save. "Jesus said to him, 'I am the way, the truth, and the life. No one comes to the Father except through Me'" (John 14:6).

You can line up every one of us on the West Coast with plans to swim to Hawaii, and no doubt, some would swim a lot farther than others. Nevertheless, we would all have one thing in common: nobody would make it! It is impossible for anybody to swim from the West Coast to Hawaii. And it is just as impossible for sinful man to make his way to a Holy God on his own without experiencing God's wrath. What one needs is a boat to get them from the West Coast to Hawaii. Moreover, the only salvation boat is the Lord Jesus Christ. That Jesus is the only way to be saved is as true as 2 + 2 = 4. There is only one answer to that equation, and there is only one way to be saved.

"Nor is there salvation in any other, for there is no other name under heaven given among men by which we must be saved" (Acts 4:12).

Facts

These are only facts. Giving mental assent to these facts is not enough to save anyone. It is not enough to give intellectual assent to these facts. We must believe and thus receive Christ.

"But as many as received Him, to them He gave the right to become children of God, to those who believe in His name" (John 1:12).

Faith

Facts must be wedded to faith. So, what do we mean when we say believe or place your faith in Christ?

Faith involves mind, emotion, and will.

Years ago, a tightrope walker named Charles Blondin, went across Niagara Falls, walking on a wire. He went back and forth. He even filled a wheelbarrow with bricks and took that across. A crowd gathered, and he asked one of them, "Do you believe I could do that with you?" The man agreed that he could. Then Blondin said, "Hop on in, and I'll carry you across." The man said, "No way!" You see, he did not really believe. He believed in his mind that Blondin could take him across; he wanted him to in his emotions, but he would not commit himself to Blondin and trust him to take him across. Saving faith involves our mind, emotion, and will.

Amazing Grace

You likely have heard the song, "Amazing Grace." We are saved by grace through faith in Jesus Christ. Now faith is not a work—faith is to believe in the work of another. "For by grace you have been saved through faith, and that not of yourselves; it is the gift of God, not of works, lest anyone should boast" (Eph. 2:8–9).

Dr. Gerstner: "Christ has done everything necessary for his salvation. Nothing now stands between the sinner and God but the sinner's good works. Nothing can keep him from Christ but his delusion that he does not need Him—that he has good works of his own that can satisfy God. If men will only be convinced that all their righteousness is as filthy rags; if men will see that there is none that does good, no, not one; if men will see that all are shut up under sin—then there will be nothing to prevent their everlasting salvation. All they need is need. All they must have is nothing. All that is required is acknowledged guilt. But alas, sinners cannot part from their virtues. They are imaginary, but they are real to them. So grace becomes unreal. The real grace of God they spurn in order to hold on to the illusory virtues of their own. Their eyes fixed on a mirage; they will not drink real water. They die of thirst in the midst of an ocean of grace."

Repentance is a synonym for faith; it is like heads and tails of *one* coin. Repentance is not making a vow you will stop sinning, nor is it a change of life. You cannot stop sinning or change your life until God saves you! I have fished most of my life and I have never cleaned a fish before I caught it. Repentance is a *change of mind*, about who you are, a sinner; and about the Lord Jesus Christ, the only one who can save you based on His death, burial, and resurrection.

Good Enough Is Not Good Enough

The religious leaders of Jesus' day prayed three times a week, fasted twice a week, never missed going to the house of worship, and memorized the Old Testament (Luke 18:9–12). Yet, Jesus said that if you are not more righteous then they, you are not going to make it!

"For I say to you, that unless your righteousness exceeds the righteousness of the scribes and

Pharisees, you will by no means enter the kingdom of heaven (Matt. 5:20).

Then he says something rather startling:

"Therefore you shall be perfect, just as your Father in heaven is perfect" (Matt. 5:48).

Did you know Jesus said it takes perfect righteousness to get to heaven? We all know that nobody is perfect! How then can we be perfectly righteous before a perfectly righteous God?

"For He made Him who knew no sin to be sin for us, that we might become the righteousness of God in Him" (2 Cor. 5:21).

The truth is, there is only one person who lived a perfect life, and that was Jesus Christ. You see, the good news is that not only did Jesus die on the cross in our place, to offer us forgiveness of all our sins, He also offers us His perfect righteousness, placed on our account! The only sin Jesus ever knew was ours; the only righteousness we will ever know is His.

Never the Same!

Salvation is not an external thing. When you receive Jesus Christ as your Savior, He makes you a new creature within!

"Therefore, if anyone is in Christ, he is a new creation; old things have passed away; behold, all things have become new" (2 Cor. 5:17).

And the Holy Spirit takes up permanent residence within you.

"And because you are sons, God has sent forth the Spirit of His Son into your hearts, crying out, 'Abba, Father'" (Gal. 4:6).

Thus, you now have the desire (new nature) and the power (indwelling Holy Spirit) to live for God. You are positionally changed from being in Adam to now being in Christ, and experientially changed because the inner transformation of regeneration and salvation begins the process of progressive sanctification, which ultimately leads to glorification.

"For it is God who works in you both to will and to do for His good pleasure" (Phil. 2:13).

While we still have an old sin nature though Satan is opposing us every step of the way, we must grow in the grace and knowledge of the Lord Jesus. It is also true that our entire life is different! If we are what we've always been, we are not saved. I know that I am saved because on the seventh of May, 1974, I received the Lord Jesus Christ as my Savior, and also because I have never gotten over it! And it is not that we are trying to be saved. If I asked you, "Are you an elephant?" You would not say, "Well, I'm trying to be!" You either are an elephant or you're not. No one who is trying to be saved understands salvation. *You are either saved or you're not!* You are saved because you have had a personal, life-changing encounter with the Lord Jesus Christ at a point in time. It is a matter of trusting not trying.

So Are You Ready to Be Saved?

If this is something you want to do, then here is a suggested prayer; the words are not what's important, but what's in your heart. If God is dealing with you, then cry out to Him:

Lord Jesus, I need you. Thank you for dying on the cross for my sins. I cannot save myself. I cannot even help you save me. But the best I know how, I confess that I am a sinner and believe that the Lord Jesus Christ died on the cross for my sins and rose from the dead. I open the door of my life and receive you right now as my Savior. Come in and make me the kind of person you want me to be.

If you just received the Lord Jesus Christ as your Savior, then you are saved! This promise is based on the authority of God's Word.

"But as many as received Him, to them He gave the right to become children of God, to those who believe in His name" (John 1:12).

A list of my other books: Go to Amazon.com and type in Johnny A Palmer Jr.

Genesis: Roots of the Nation Vol. 1

Genesis: Roots of the Nation Vol. 2

Genesis: Roots of the Nation Vol. 3

Exodus: Redemption of the Nation. Vol. 1

Exodus: Redemption of the Nation. Vol. 2

Book of Leviticus

Book of Judges

First Samuel

Second Samuel

Book of Job

The Gospel of Mark: the servant.

The Gospel of Luke Vol. 1

The Gospel of Luke Vol. 2

The Gospel of Luke Vol. 3

The Gospel of Luke Vol. 4

The Book of Acts

Ephesians: A Manual for Survival

Jude: Hey Jude

Revelation: The Revelation of Jesus Christ

A Manual for Revival

Practical Principles for Studying the Bible

Read Limit 30 mph

Proclamations from a Politically Incorrect Prophet

Elvis Wellness

Awake for the Dawn is About to Break

Rewards of Rejecting Christ

Which Messiah will you Meet?

GPS-23

Spiritual Survivor Man

A Father's Day Message

A Mother's Day Message

I'm For Life

Double Solitaire with the Trinity

Fuel – The Lord's Prayer

Made in the USA
Lexington, KY
07 February 2018